At Issue

| America's Infrastructure

Other Books in the At Issue Series

At Issue

America's Infrastructure

Lisa Idzikowski, Book Editor

GREENHAVEN
PUBLISHING

Published in 2019 by Greenhaven Publishing, LLC
353 3rd Avenue, Suite 255, New York, NY 10010

First Edition

Articles in Greenhaven Publishing anthologies are often edited for length to meet page
requirements. In addition, original titles of these works are changed to clearly present
the main thesis and to explicitly indicate the author's opinion. Every effort is made to
ensure that Greenhaven Publishing accurately reflects the original intent of the authors.
Every effort has been made to trace the owners of the copyrighted material.

Cover image: trekandshoot/Shutterstock.com

Library of Congress Cataloging-in-Publication Data

Names: Idzikowski, Lisa, editor.
Title: America's infrastructure / Lisa Idzikowski, book editor.
Description: New York : Greenhaven Publishing, [2019] | Series: At issue |
  Audience: Grade 9 to 12. | Includes bibliographical references and index.
Identifiers: LCCN 2018022302| ISBN 9781534504165 (library bound) | ISBN
  9781534504431 (pbk.)
Subjects: LCSH: Infrastructure (Economics)—United States—Juvenile
  literature. | Government spending policy—United States—Juvenile
  literature.
Classification: LCC HC110.C3 A5394 2019 | DDC 363.60973—dc23
LC record available at https://lccn.loc.gov/2018022302

Manufactured in the United States of America

Website: http://greenhavenpublishing.com

Contents

Introduction

> "Renewing the nation's infrastructure and solving our problems will take collective action. Leaders from all levels of government and the private sector, along with every American, must prioritize closing our infrastructure deficit, commit to a future in which we improve infrastructure, and value it as key to our quality of life and economic prosperity. Every day of delay escalates our shared costs, jeopardizes our health, and risks our security—an option our country, economy and communities can no longer afford."
>
> —Former president of the American Society of Civil Engineers, Greg DiLoreto, in the 2017 ASCE Infrastructure Report Card

Infrastructure, according to *Merriam-Webster*, "is the underlying structure of a country and its economy, the fixed installations that it needs in order to function. These include roads, bridges, dams, the water and sewer systems, railways and subways, airports, and harbors." Most Americans use some or multiple forms of infrastructure on a daily basis and may take this system for granted. Highways, subways, airplanes, bridges, and public transportation get them to work or school or pretty much anywhere else they might need to go. Water and sewer systems usually provide clean water, and the electrical grid powers everything from digital equipment to the coffee makers used to make people's favorite morning cup.

It may be easy not to think of infrastructure until something malfunctions, breaks down, or is destroyed, but it is also true that many people are concerned and interested in the topic. Amid the 2017 US presidential campaign, the top two candidates—Hillary Clinton and Donald Trump—made campaign promises about rebuilding America's infrastructure. Clinton promised to "boost federal investment [in infrastructure] by $275 billion over the next five years," and to make sure that by 2020, all Americans had affordable access to the internet.[1] After being elected, President Donald Trump promised Americans that

> *we are going to fix our inner cities and rebuild our highways, bridges, tunnels, airports, schools. Hospitals. We're going to rebuild our infrastructure, which will become, by the way, second to none. And we will put millions of our people to work as we rebuild it.*[2]

Various polls conducted before, during, and after the campaign demonstrate that Americans are concerned about the country's infrastructure and want it fixed and improved. A Gallup poll in spring of 2016 showed that 75% of those polled agreed that the federal government should spend more money to fix the country's infrastructure,[3] and a spring 2017 poll by CNN demonstrated that 79% of surveyed Americans favor a boost in infrastructure spending.[4]

Professionals are also concerned about the condition of American infrastructure. Since 1998, and every four years thereafter, the American Society of Civil Engineers (ASCE) has issued and published a report card detailing the state of American infrastructure. Sixteen categories of public works including aviation, bridges, dams, drinking water, energy, hazardous waste, inland waterways, levees, ports, public parks and recreation, rail, roads, schools, solid waste, transit, and wastewater systems are judged on performance and capacity, and then given a letter grade. From an average score of "D" in 1998, to the latest "D+" in 2017, according to civil engineers America's infrastructure "is aging, underperforming, and in need of sustained care and action."[5]

Not surprisingly, the topic of America's infrastructure swirls in controversy. While the ASCE strongly suggests that the system is in dire shape and that upgrades, improvements, and investments must be made, other groups and individuals dispute the ASCE's findings. These controversies take many forms: proponents insist on building, expanding, repairing, and upgrading America's infrastructure system. Arguments for additional work cite a variety of lost opportunities if the US doesn't fix its infrastructure, prepare for future needs, and remain competitive with the rest of the world. According to the ASCE, the US stands to suffer "$7 trillion in lost business sales by 2025; and 2.5 million lost American jobs (and) on top of those costs, hardworking American families will lose upwards of $3,400 in disposable income each year – about $9 each day."

Opponents argue that the US is still ahead of many developed countries in infrastructure condition, maintenance, and reliability. Arguments against additional work also focus on the economics of the issue—the ASCE projects a spending gap on infrastructure needs through 2025 of close to 2 trillion dollars—and who is going to pay that hard-to-imagine price tag? A consensus seems to agree that some form of joint venture between federal, state, city, municipal, and private groups will be the only way to tackle this immense monetary necessity.

It's very hard to argue against either side in this controversy. An almost unimaginable amount of money needs to be dedicated to infrastructure planning, development, and insight for the future. Whether this becomes necessary from normal wear and tear, damage from once-in-a-century storms that could be caused by climate change, or the transition to "smart" infrastructure systems, it is clear that in time changes will need to be made to infrastructure. American politicians may have to become bold leaders and step up to the challenges and make the right decisions as President Dwight D. Eisenhower did when he created the national highway system in 1955, stating that "Together, the united forces of our communication and transportation systems are dynamic elements in the very name we bear—United States. Without them, we would be a mere alliance of many separate parts." Additionally, the American public may also be forced to step up and assist in paying for infrastructure and demand its improvement.

US citizens can't sit in their living rooms and watch the nightly news reports of another bridge collapse like the one in Minneapolis, Minnesota in August of 2007. And they can't passively or numbly scroll through news feeds on their phones past another infrastructure disaster story like the water debacle of Flint, Michigan of 2016. Many knowledgeable individuals agree that up-to-date infrastructure is a necessity for the safety and well-being of all US citizens, and that the challenges and problems must be tackled and not put off for future generations to handle.

The current debate that surrounds the issue of infrastructure is explored in *At Issue: America's Infrastructure* through a wide variety of perspectives, shedding light on this divisive and ongoing contemporary issue.

Notes

1. "Americans Say 'Yes' to Spending More on VA, Infrastructure," by Frank Newport, Gallup News, March 21, 2016. http://news.gallup.com/poll/190136/americans-say-yes-spending-infrastructure.aspx.

2. "Trump looks to revitalize infrastructure push with New York meeting," by Dan Merica, CNN Politics, August 15, 2016. https://www.cnn.com/2017/08/15/politics/trump-infrastructure/index.html.

3. "Americans Say 'Yes' to Spending More on VA, Infrastructure," by Frank Newport, Gallup News, March 21, 2016. http://news.gallup.com/poll/190136/americans-say-yes-spending-infrastructure.aspx.

4. "CNN/ORC poll: Most back boost in infrastructure spending, oppose growing military budget," by Jennifer Agiesta, CNN Politics, March 8, 2017. https://www.cnn.com/2017/03/08/politics/donald-trump-poll-spending-defense-infrastructure/index.html.

5. "2017 Infrastructure Report Card," ASCE. https://www.infrastructurereportcard.org.

1

A Quick Look at Roads of the Past and Bridges of the Present

Henry Petroski

Henry Petroski is an engineer, a professor of civil engineering and history at Duke Univeristy, and an author. His latest book is The Road Taken: The History and Future of America's Infrastructure.

This viewpoint provides an introduction to the subject of infrastructure and the built environment by focusing on roads and bridges. It explores the documentation of the history of these two structure types. The viewpoint looks at research performed by Henry Petroski to examine at the role of the federal and local government in infrastructure over time, arguing that greater accountability and public investment are necessary for future infrastructure-related projects.

I nfrastructure makes modern civilization possible. Roads, power grids, sewage systems and water networks all underpin society as we know it, forming the basis of our built environment ... at least when they work.

As Henry Petroski documents in *The Road Taken: The History and Future of America's Infrastructure*, physical infrastructure in the United States is in an ongoing state of crisis. The American Society of Civil Engineers recently give American roads and

"Public Works: Rethinking America's Transportation Infrastructure," Henry Petroski, September 6, 2016. Reprinted by permission.

bridges dismal letter grades of D and C+ respectively. Their report describes roughly sixty-five thousand bridges in the United States as being "structurally deficient."

Petroski, a professor of civil engineering and history at Duke University, notes that while the concept of infrastructure is universal our current use of word itself is actually relatively new. In America, the old phrase "public works" became associated with pork barrel spending and fell out of favor in the latter half of the 20th century. Politicians had developed a reputation for swapping favors and funds for support on public works legislation, trading votes and cash to get things done.

Infrastructure graft and corruption peaked publicly on October 10, 1973 when Spiro Agnew became the second Vice President to resign the office. His resignation came in the wake of a bribery scandal. These bribes were *not* tied to his federal position but rather to his time has governor of Maryland and infrastructure projects he was illegally paid to promote in office. In fact, Agnew was in a much greater position to participate in such schemes as a state official rather than a federal one: states and municipalities are largely responsible for roads in the United States.

Article 1, Section 8 of the US Constitution states that the federal government can build "post roads" (meaning routes for the post office to operate effectively) but no other kinds of roads are specified. When a bill in was passed by Congress in 1817 that approved the funding of internal improvements in the country (like roads and canals) it was vetoed by then President James Madison because he saw it as unconstitutional. While the federal government cannot take charge of state roadway and bridge projects, it does provide a level of support and standardization (in part by leveraging national gas taxes).

Standards for center lines, for example, help keep lanes apart while side lines help drivers stay on the road at night. Keeping these the same from state to state makes interstate driving smoother.

Originally roads had no lines at all, leading drivers to hug the center and contributing to head-on collisions. Over time, standardized solutions helped make driving safer both locally and nationally.

Likewise with numbering systems, the federal government has played a significant (albeit less physical) role. East-West highways are assigned even numbers and North-South highways are given odd ones, all of which helps people navigate within and beyond a given state. Three-digit numbers for interstate highway beltways let drivers know they are on a loop, neither N/S or E/W (e.g. I-494 circles around Minneapolis, connecting to East-West I-94 above and below the city).

The federal government also helps the highway network by giving money to states to assist with ongoing construction and repairs. Unfortunately, the gasoline tax, which feeds a highway trust fund, hasn't been keeping up with the needs of the national road network.

In a sense, the federal government is working against itself: it relies on gasoline to generate needed funds but is also encouraging fuel-efficient electric and hybrid vehicles, which consume less gas. The gas tax has also not been raised since 1993, reinforcing the problem.

States are thus facing tough choices about what to do on a local level. Some are increasing state-specific gas taxes to compensate. Others are implementing special taxes (e.g. per mile) on efficient vehicles in an attempt to get more money from more fuel-efficient cars and trucks.

The cycle of politics, at both local and national levels, also contributes to short-term thinking with respect to road and bridge infrastructure projects. Asphalt, for instance, has a shorter lifespan than concrete, but politicians looking at the next few years tend to opt for the former over the latter due in part due to cost.

Some municipalities are even un-paving roads, reverting them to dirt and gravel, as a cost-saving measure. For low-traffic roads, this can work from an engineering point of view, though the sustainability of the practice is questionable. Also, it can annoy citizens, kicking up dust and slowing down drives.

Some communities are particularly conscientious about infrastructure. Small towns responsible for their own roads, for instance, often pay closer attention and know the parties in play (local contractors).

Even in larger cities, critical infrastructure failures can lead to fast, decisive and effective action. When the I-35W bridge collapsed in Minneapolis, Minnesota, a replacement bridge was put in place on budget and on time. On the one hand, the turnaround was impressive. On the other hand, it underscores the crisis of American infrastructure.

Aside from simple stability, there are also questions of aesthetics and costs when it comes to things like signature bridges. The Golden Gate in San Francisco is quite beautiful but it also came in on budget.

Nearby, however, the recently rebuilt East Bay span of the Bay Bridge is arguably a nice work of design and engineering, but its expressive form has contributed to budget overages. Anything that is fundamentally new and different tends to add costs, in part because it requires working out novel solutions on the engineering side of things.

In some cases, it is hard to say in advance whether a more sophisticated design will pay off, but another California bridge shows that it can. The Sundial Bridge appears to have been worth the added investment. This cable-stayed bridge for bicycles and pedestrians spans the Sacramento River in Redding and forms a giant sundial. It was designed by starchitect Santiago Calatrava and completed in 2004.

While it cost a controversial sum of $23,000,000 (nearly ten times the initial budget), post-construction analysis suggests it may have been a wise choice in light of tourism dollars generated. In the fiscal year following its opening, the adjacent Turtle Bay Exploration Park saw a 42-percent increase in its visitation. In 2011, Redding's city manager stated that the bridge "continues to generate millions of dollars' worth of commerce and tourism each year."

In theory, infrastructure is a bipartisan issue – everyone wants roads and bridges to be nice, safe and smooth. In practice, big infrastructure projects tend to go over budget and lack accountability. Arguably this is both a political and cultural issue: we as a nation need to become more invested in our infrastructure, financially and emotionally. Perhaps it is time to reclaim the term "public works" as a reminder to politicians and citizens alike that these projects are undertaken by and for the people.

2

Infrastructure and Its Supporting Institutions Must Both Be Redesigned

Thaddeus R. Miller

Thaddeus R. Miller is an assistant professor at Arizona State University. In a recent book, Reconstructing Sustainability Science: Knowledge and Action for a Sustainable Future, *Miller looks at how scientists can make the link between knowledge and social action.*

Thaddeus R. Miller argues that infrastructure and the institutions that support it must be changed, updated, and maintained for them to continue functioning in the future. Miller asserts that systems must be reworked and made resilient and flexible because of the recent pattern of extreme weather events, which will only become more commonplace in the future. Through looking at the case of Hurricane Harvey in 2017, Miller explores the ways in which extreme weather events impact infrastructure and how engineers propose updating infrastructure to account for such events.

Before Hurricane Harvey made landfall on Aug. 25, there was little doubt that its impact would be devastating and wide-ranging.

Unfortunately, Harvey delivered and then some with early estimates of the damage at over US$190 billion, which would make it the costliest storm in U.S. history. The rain dumped on the Houston area by Harvey has been called "unprecedented," making engineering and floodplain design standards look outdated at best and irresponsible at worst.

But to dismiss this as a once-in-a-lifetime event would be a mistake. With more very powerful storms forming in the Atlantic this hurricane season, we should know better. We must listen to those telling a more complicated story, one that involves decades of land use planning and poor urban design that has generated impervious surfaces at a fantastic pace.

As the Houston region turns its attention to rebuilding and other cities consider ramping up efforts to make their infrastructure more resilient, it is this story that can provide valuable lessons for policymakers, planners, engineers, developers and the public. These lessons are all the more important against the backdrop of a Trump administration that has stripped requirements for infrastructure projects to consider climate impacts and may try to offer an infrastructure investment package.

We draw from our research as a social scientist and an engineer and from our experience helping to lead the Urban Resilience to Extreme Weather Events Sustainability Research Network (funded by the U.S. National Science Foundation). Here are six rules for investing in infrastructure for the 21st century that recognize the need to rethink how we design and operate our infrastructure.

If we design with the technologies, needs and climate conditions of the 20th century, we will no longer serve society and the hazards we will encounter now and in the future.

A Strong Foundation

Proactive Maintenance First

In 2017, U.S. infrastructure was given a D+ by the American Society for Civil Engineering Infrastructure Report Card. The bill to repair all those deteriorating roads, bridges and dams would tally $210 billion by 2020, and $520 billion in 2040. For example, the US Army Corps of Engineers estimates there are 15,460 dams in the U.S. with "high" hazard ratings.

Yet, when our cities and states spend on infrastructure, it is too often on new infrastructure projects. And new infrastructure tends to emulate the models, designs and standards that we've used for decades – for instance, more highway capacity or new pipelines.

Meanwhile, resources for long-term maintenance are often lacking, resulting in a race to scrape together funding to keep systems running. If we want to get serious about avoiding disasters in a rapidly changing world, we must get serious about the maintenance of existing infrastructure.

Invest In and Redesign Institutions, Not Just Infrastructure

When analyzing breakdowns in infrastructure, it is tempting to blame the technical design. Yet design parameters are set by institutions and shaped by politics, financing and policy goals.

So failures in infrastructure are not just technical failures; they are institutional ones as well. They are failures in "knowledge systems," or the ability to generate, communicate and utilize knowledge within and across institutions.

For example, the levee failures during Hurricane Katrina are often interpreted as technical failures. They were, but we also knew the levees would fail in a storm as powerful as Katrina. And so the levee failures were also failures in institutional design – the information about the weakness of the levees was not utilized in part because the Hurricane Protection System was poorly funded and lacked the necessary institutional and political power to force action.

In the wake of Harvey, basic design and floodplain development parameters, like the 100-year flood, are being acknowledged as fundamentally flawed. Our ability to design more resilient infrastructure will depend on our ability to design more effective institutions to manage these complex problems, learn from failures and adapt.

Resilience and Uncertainty

Design for Climate Change

When it comes to infrastructure's ability to handle more extreme events that are predicted to come with climate change, the primary problem is not bad engineering or faulty technical designs. Instead, it's that infrastructure are typically sized based on the intensity and frequency of historical events. Yet these historical conditions are now routinely exceeded: since 1979, Houston alone has experienced three 500-year storms.

Climate change will make preparing for future storms much harder. These events are not just associated with precipitation and inland flooding but include more extreme heat, cold, drought, wildfires, coastal flooding and wind. Buildings, roads, water networks and other infrastructure last decades and designing for historical events may result in more frequent failure as events become more frequent or intense with climate change. Infrastructure designers and managers must shift from risk-based to resilience-based thinking, so that our systems can better withstand and bounce back from these extreme events.

Manage Infrastructure as Interconnected and Interdependent

In his 1987 essay, "Atchafalaya," writer John McPhee explores efforts by the U.S. Army Corps of Engineers to control the Atchafalaya and Mississippi River systems. He brilliantly showed that rather than bringing predictability to a complex and meandering riverine system, the Old River Control system created unpredictability. "It's a mixture of hydrologic events and human events… This is planned chaos… Nobody knows where it's going to end."

While floodplain management has made advances since then, the impact of development and infrastructure design is still often considered on a piecemeal basis. As Montgomery County engineer Mark Mooney noted in a recent Houston Chronicle article, "I can show you on any individual project how runoff has been properly mitigated. Having said that, when you see the increase in impervious surfaces that we have, it's clear the way water moves through our county has changed. It's all part of a massive puzzle everyone is trying to sort out."

Infrastructure planning and design must consider the legacy of past decisions and how risks build up over time as ecological, technological and human systems interact in increasingly uncertain and complex ways.

Infrastructure and Equity

Create Flexible Infrastructure

Given that our infrastructures are centralized and satisfy demands that don't change rapidly (we use water and electricity much in the way we did over the past century), they tend to be inflexible. Yet we need our urban systems and the infrastructure that support them to be resilient. And flexibility is a necessary precondition for resilience.

Current designs favor robustness and redundancy. These infrastructure tend to be difficult to change and the managing institutions are often structured and constrained in ways that create barriers to flexibility. Consider the difference in flexibility of landline versus mobile phones, in terms of both use and changing the hardware. Similarly, new strategies are needed to incorporate flexibility into our infrastructure. In the case of hurricanes, roadways with smart signaling and controls that dynamically adjust stoplights and reverse lanes to allow vehicles to evacuate quickly would be of significant value.

Design Infrastructure for Everyone

Large disasters almost always highlight systemic social inequalities in our communities, as we saw in the 1995 Chicago heat wave, Hurricane Katrina and now Hurricane Harvey.

Yet as cities rebuild and other cities watch to glean lessons, we consistently sidestep the historical legacies, public policies and political-economic structures that continue to make low-income and minority populations, such as homeless people, more vulnerable to extreme weather events. For this to change, infrastructure must be designed with the most vulnerable in mind first.

Too often the services delivered by climate-resilient infrastructure are first built for the communities that have the economic and political power to demand them, resulting in what some have called ecological gentrification. Policymakers and planners must engage diverse communities and ensure that infrastructure services are designed for everyone – and communities need to demand it.

3

Infrastructure Suffers Because Not Everyone Pays a Fair Share of Taxes

Chuck Collins

Chuck Collins is a researcher and writer based at the Institute for Policy Studies. He writes extensively on the topic of income inequality in America.

Chuck Collins was once part of the "super-rich billionaire club" in America before he gave it all up. Now he researches and writes extensively about income inequality and the related issues it creates. In this viewpoint, Collins outlines the business of tax evasion and why America's infrastructure is suffering because the super-rich refuse to pay their fair share of taxes. Without proper taxation, the government does not have adequate funds to support large-scale infrastructure projects, and all Americans suffer as a result.

If you find yourself traveling this summer, take a closer look at America's deteriorating infrastructure — our crumbling roads, sidewalks, public parks, and train and bus stations.

Government officials will tell us "there's no money" to repair or properly maintain our tired infrastructure. Nor do we want to raise taxes, they say.

But what if billions of dollars in tax revenue have gone missing?

New research suggests that the super-rich are hiding their money at alarming rates. A study by economists Annette

"What Happened to America's Wealth? The Rich Hid It," by Chuck Collins, CounterPunch, June 29, 2017. Reprinted by permission.

Alstadsaeter, Niels Johannesen, and Gabriel Zucman reports that households with wealth over $40 million evade 25 to 30 percent of personal income and wealth taxes.

These stunning numbers have two troubling implications.

First, we're missing billions in taxes each year. That's partly why our roads and transit systems are falling apart.

Second, wealth inequality may be even worse than we thought. Economic surveys estimate that roughly 85 percent of income and wealth gains in the last decade have gone to the wealthiest one-tenth of the top 1 percent.

That's bad enough. But what if the concentration is even greater?

Visualize the nation's wealth as an expansive and deep reservoir of fresh water. A small portion of this water provides sustenance to fields and villages downstream, in the form of tax dollars for public services.

In recent years, the water level has declined to a trickle, and the villages below are suffering from water shortages. Everyone is told to tighten their belts and make sacrifices.

Deep below the water surface, however, is a hidden pipe, siphoning vast amounts of water — as much as a third of the whole reservoir — off to a secret pool in the forest.

The rich are swimming while the villagers go thirsty and the fields dry up.

Yes, there are vast pools of privately owned wealth, mostly held by a small segment of super-rich Americans. The wealthiest 400 billionaires have at least as much wealth as 62 percent of the U.S. population — that's nearly *200 million* of us.

Don't taxpayers of all incomes under-report their incomes? Maybe here and there.

But these aren't folks making a few dollars "under the table." These are billionaires stashing away trillions of the world's wealth. The latest study underscores that tax evasion by the super-rich is at least 10 times greater — and in some nations 250 times more likely — than by everyone else.

How is that possible? After all, most of us have our taxes taken out of our paychecks and pay sales taxes at the register. Homeowners get their house assessed and pay a property tax.

But the wealthy have the resources to hire the services of what's called the "wealth defense industry." These aren't your "mom and pop" financial advisers that sell life insurance or help folks plan for retirement.

The wealth defenders of the super-rich — including tax lawyers, estate planners, accountants, and other financial professionals — are accomplices in the heist. They drive the getaway cars, by designing complex trusts, shell companies, and offshore accounts to hide money.

These managers help the private jet set avoid paying their fair share of taxes, even as they disproportionately benefit from living in a country with the rule of law, property rights protections, and public infrastructure the rest of us pay for.

Not all wealthy are tax dodgers. A group called the Patriotic Millionaires advocates for eliminating loopholes and building a fair and transparent tax system. They're pressing Congress to crack down on tax evasion by the superrich.

Their message: Bring the wealth home! Stop hiding the wealth in offshore accounts and complicated trusts. Pay your fair share to the support the public services and protections that we all enjoy.

4

US Infrastructure Must Be Improved and Maintained

The White House

This report was prepared for the White House by the National Economic Council and the President's Council of Economic Advisers

The report detailed in this viewpoint was commissioned by the White House and analyzes the key issues surrounding the infrastructure of US roads and highways. Beginning with a very brief historical look at the start of the national highway system, which was requested by President Eisenhower, the report continues on to today's network of transportation. The viewpoint focuses on the reasons why infrastructure should be improved and maintained and speaks to the various economic and societal benefits to be gained from improved infrastructure.

A high quality transportation network is vital to a top performing economy. Investments by previous generations of Americans – from the Erie Canal in 1807, to the Transcontinental Railroad in 1869, to the Interstate Highway System in the 1950s and 1960s – were instrumental in putting the country on a path for sustained economic growth, productivity increases, an unrivalled national market for good and services, and international competitiveness. But today, current estimates indicate that America's transportation

"An Economic Analysis Of Transportation Infrastructure Investment," The White House, July 2014.

infrastructure is not keeping pace with demands or the needs of our growing economy, for today or for future generations.

A well-performing transportation network keeps jobs in America, allows businesses to expand, and lowers prices on household goods to American families. It allows businesses to manage their inventories and transport goods more cheaply and efficiently as well as access a variety of suppliers and markets for their products, making it more cost-effective for manufacturers to keep production in or move production to the United States. American families benefit too: as consumers, from lower priced goods; and as workers, by gaining better access to jobs.

The economic benefits of smart infrastructure investment are long-term competitiveness, productivity, innovation, lower prices, and higher incomes, while infrastructure investment also creates many thousands of American jobs in the near-term.

- Today there are more than 4 million miles of road, 600,000 bridges, and 3,000 transit providers in the U.S. And yet, over the past 20 years, total federal, state, and local investment in transportation has fallen as a share of GDP – while population, congestion, and maintenance backlogs have increased.
- The U.S. lags behind many of its overseas competitors in transportation infrastructure investment. In the most recent World Economic Forum rankings, the U.S. had in less than a decade fallen from 7th to 18th overall in the quality of our roads.
- 65 percent of America's major roads are rated in less than good condition, one in four bridges require significant repair or cannot handle today's traffic, and forty five percent of Americans lack access to transit.

The costs of inadequate infrastructure investment are exhibited all around us. Americans spend 5.5 billion hours in traffic each year, costing families more than $120 billion in extra fuel and lost time. American businesses pay $27 billion a year in extra freight transportation costs, increasing shipping delays and raising prices on everyday products. Underinvestment impacts safety too. There were more than 33,000 traffic fatalities last year alone and roadway conditions are a significant factor in approximately one-third of traffic fatalities. Such fatalities occur disproportionately in rural America, in part because of inadequate road conditions.

That's why the President introduced the GROW AMERICA Act, a four-year, $302 billion proposal to fund our nation's transportation system and invest in the nation's future growth. The President's plan addresses the nation's significant infrastructure investment gap through targeted investments now and lays the groundwork for increased efficiency in the future. The President has been pressing Congress to act to avoid a lapse in funding of the Highway Trust Fund which will go insolvent as early as August, putting numerous active projects at risk.

Long Term Economic Benefits from Infrastructure Investment

A modern transportation network is vital to our economy, and is a prerequisite for future growth. President Eisenhower's vision is even more relevant today than it was in 1955, when he said in his State of the Union Address, "A modern, efficient highway system is essential to meet the needs of our growing population, our expanding economy, and our national security."

Today, that vision includes making not only our nation's highways, but its entire infrastructure system, more efficient and effective. A well-performing transportation network allows businesses to manage inventories and transport goods more cheaply, access a variety of suppliers and markets for their products, and get employees reliably to work. American families benefit too: as consumers, from lower priced goods, and as workers, by gaining better access to jobs. An efficient transportation network also enables firms and people to locate near one another, so that they can benefit from shared access to inputs of production, an insight first recognized in the 1890s.[1] This is all the more vital as regional economies with interdependent urban, suburban and rural areas relying on each other for innovation, employment, and growth become more important in manufacturing, energy, tourism, technology, and other US industries.

Evaluating how transportation and other infrastructure benefit the overall economy has been the subject of extensive economic literature. David Aschauer's research found very large economic gains from public capital generally (including but not limited to transportation), suggesting $1 in output gains for $1 in increased investment.[2] Subsequent research has detected more modest effects that can be sensitive to the types of public capital, sectors of the economy, geography level, and time periods considered as well as methods employed to study the data.[3]

More recent research has highlighted the importance of selecting investments wisely in key areas of the country on the basis of their economic contributions. This research has also emphasized the importance of maintaining existing assets in a good state of repair.[4] Beyond contributions to economic growth and productivity, quality transportation infrastructure can also benefit businesses and consumers alike through shorter and more reliable travel times, resulting in direct and indirect benefits that ripple throughout the economy.

Less Road Congestion
A well-connected transportation network means faster, more reliable travel times for both people and goods. Providing transportation choices enables businesses to choose the most efficient way to ship their goods. It is also important, because time spent stuck in traffic not only wastes fuel, resulting in higher out of pocket costs for businesses and households, but also wastes time that could be spent engaged in more productive activities.

For example, the Texas Transportation Institute estimates that American commuters in urban areas collectively lost 5.5 billion hours stuck in traffic in 2011, meaning the average commuter lost nearly a week to traffic. TTI's calculations further suggest that traffic congestion caused American commuters to purchase an extra 2.9 billion gallons of fuel, costing them more than $120 billion in added fuel costs and wasted time.[5] Further, well-maintained roads, coupled with access to public transportation and other driving alternatives, can lower traffic congestion and accident rates which not only save Americans time and money but also save lives.

More Reliable Shipments and Travel Times

More congestion also means that both businesses and families must account for the unreliability of travel times when making their plans. For the trucking industry alone, the Federal Highway Administration calculates that highway bottlenecks cause more than 243 million hours of delay each year, at a cost of $7.8 billion annually.[6] Moreover, when shipping takes longer, businesses must re-orient their supply chains, hold more inventories, or rely on more distribution centers, resulting in added costs. To cite just a few examples, in a 2005 survey of Portland, Oregon business leaders, the Economic Development Research Group and found that:

- Intel moved their last shipment departure time up two hours for out-bound shipments to avoid peak-period congestion.
- Sysco Foods opened a new regional distribution center in Spokane to better serve their market area (because it was taking too long to serve its market from the Portland area). Providence Health Systems planned to relocate its warehousing and support operations because medical deliveries were requiring more than four hours in some cases.
- OrePac increased inventories by seven to eight percent because of congestion delays, siphoning of resources that could have been used for other investment.
- PGE estimated that it spent approximately $500,000 a year for additional travel time for its maintenance crews.[7]

Similarly, other researchers have found:

- Nike must spend an additional $4 million per week to carry an extra 7-to-14 days of inventory to compensate for shipping delays.[8]
- One day of delay requires American President Line's eastbound trans- Pacific services to increase its use of containers and chassis by 1,300, which adds $4 million in costs per year.[9]
- A week-long disruption to container movements through the Ports of Los Angeles and Long Beach could cost the national economy between $65 and $150 million per day.

Higher Land Values and Local Economic Development

Transportation investments affect not only the level of economic output but geographic distribution of economic activity. Declining transportation costs in the past facilitated the growth of cities across the United States. Chicago, for example, grew in size and importance because it served as a central hub between the fruitful plains of the mid-west and the markets of the northeast and Europe.

Infrastructure investment can also raise property values, particularly if these investments bring about improvements in local living standards (including shorter commute times and greater proximity to desirable amenities).[10] For example, research suggests that proximity to public transit raises the value of residential and commercial real estate. Bernard Weinstein studied the effect of the Dallas light rail system on property values, and found that a jump in total valuations around light rail stations was about 25 percent greater than in similar neighborhoods not served by the system.[11] This is consistent with studies conducted in St. Louis,[12] Chicago,[13] Sacramento,[14] and San Diego,[15] all of which find that property values experience a premium effect when located near public transit systems.

Immediate Job Creation in Key Industries

While the most important economic impact of smart infrastructure investment comes from long-term competitiveness, productivity, innovation, lower prices, and higher incomes, infrastructure investment also creates many thousands of jobs in the near-term that are directly linked to the American economy and difficult to ship overseas. These jobs span across a wide variety of different industries. For example, road building not only requires construction workers, but also grading and paving equipment, gasoline or diesel to run the machines, smaller hand tools of all sorts, raw inputs of cement, gravel, and asphalt, surveyors to map the site, engineers and site managers, and even accountants to keep track of costs.

Analysis of data from the BEA 2012 annual input-output table and related data from the Bureau of Labor Statistics (BLS) suggests that 68 percent of the jobs created by investing in infrastructure are in the construction sector, 10 percent in the manufacturing sector, and 6 percent in retail trade.

Construction and manufacturing sectors were disproportionately affected by the economic crisis – so infrastructure investments help support hard-hit American workers. Although the construction sector has added 186,000 jobs over the last 12 months, the unemployment rate for construction workers remains elevated at 9.9 percent (based on a twelve-month moving average of not seasonally adjusted data). At the same time, the number of construction jobs has fallen by nearly 20 percent since December 2007. Accelerated infrastructure investment would provide an opportunity for construction workers to productively apply their skills and experience.

Investing in infrastructure now would not only help those workers for whom unemployment remains unacceptably high, but would also allow state and localities to address their critical needs at a time when costs for building and financing projects are very low. Specifically, the costs of borrowing through the issuance of municipal bonds are at historic lows. Bond revenues are the primary source of infrastructure finance at the state and local level—and are also used to match federal funds.

Construction costs for highways have declined more than 20 percent since before the 2007 recession and have been relatively flat since 2011. Moreover, 20-year bond yields remain below pre-recessionary levels, but as the economy continues to recover and prices begin to rise, higher construction costs and bond-yields will likely follow.

Investing in infrastructure provides short term benefits to states and localities to address their critical needs at a time when borrowing costs are low but future revenues are uncertain. State and local governments are significant partners in funding public infrastructure. During recessions, it is common for state and local governments to cut back on capital projects – such as building schools, roads, and parks – in order to meet balanced budget requirements. Although state revenues have now regained pre-recession levels, growth has been moderate.[16] Past research has also found that expenditures on capital projects are more than four times as sensitive to year- to-year fluctuations in state income as is state spending in general.[17] Providing additional federal support for transportation infrastructure investment would be prudent given the ongoing budgetary pressures facing state and local governments.

Infrastructure Impacts on American Families

Investing in transportation and providing more high-quality transportation choices provides American families with options to save time and money, so that they can retain more of their income for other purposes and spend more time doing what they want, rather than spending time getting there.

Lower Household Costs

For the average American family, transportation expenditures rank second only to housing expenditures. Given how much Americans spend on transportation, public investments which lower the cost of transportation could have a meaningful impact on families' budgets. Reducing fuel consumption, decreasing the need for car maintenance due to poor road conditions, and increasing the availability of affordable and accessible public transportation systems would allow Americans to spend less money on transportation.

Transportation expenditures can be particularly burdensome for middle class families. For the 90 percent of Americans below the top decile in the income distribution, transportation costs absorb one out of every seven dollars of income. Transportation expenses relative to income are almost twice as great for the bottom 90 percent as they are for the top 10 percent.

Vehicle Operating and Maintenance Costs

Moreover, improving our nation's transportation system can save American families money by reducing the costs associated with congestion and the additional wear and tear caused by poor road conditions. TRIP, an industry group, notes that deteriorated roads accelerate the depreciation of vehicles and the need for repairs because the stress on the vehicle increases in proportion to the level of roughness of the pavement surface. Similarly, tire wear and fuel consumption increase as roads deteriorate since there is less efficient transfer of power to the drive train and additional friction between the road and the tires. They estimate the average motorist in the U.S. pays $377 each year in additional vehicle operating costs as a result of driving on roads in need of repair, which varies by major urbanized area.

Health and Safety

More road congestion also means more stop-and-go traffic which leads to harmful emissions. According to the Environmental Protection Agency, transportation accounts for one-third of all carbon dioxide emissions from fossil fuel combustion, and these emissions are particularly harmful to children's health.[18]

But the impact of the transportation system on our health also extends beyond traffic crashes and air quality to American families' fundamental quality of life. In 2010, the Gallup-Healthways Well-Being Index found that 40 percent of employees who spend more than 90 minutes getting home from work "experienced worry for much of the previous day." That number falls to 28 percent for those with "negligible" commutes of 10 minutes or less. The survey also found that one in three workers with a 90-minute daily commute has recurrent neck or back problems. This only confirms what 900 Texan women expressed in 2006, when Nobel laureate Daniel Kahneman and Princeton economist Alan Krueger asked them how much they enjoyed a number of frequent activities. Commuting came in dead last.

Current Budgetary Climate

Since the 1950s, the Highway Trust Fund has been the primary federal source of funding for state and local surface transportation projects. Every five to ten years, Congress authorized predictable levels of funding to states and later local transit agencies for road, bridge, and transit projects. And over the last quarter-century, Congress has customarily taken stock on the nation's needs for transportation investment and has authorized multi-year funding increases of roughly 40 percent over the prior authorization to better meet the needs of our communities and our economy.

But over the past few years, revenues that go into the Fund haven't kept pace with the federal funding levels promised to states by Congress. As a result, the Department of Transportation projects the Highway Trust Fund to be insolvent by the end of this summer. Soon afterwards, Congressional authorities for the federal government to reimburse states and localities for spending on surface transportation – including roads, highways, and transit – will expire.

The President has called on Congress to ensure the continuity of the Highway Trust Fund in the near-term, and to reauthorize transportation legislation on a long-term basis with substantially increased funding levels to give States, communities and businesses the certainty to invest, as many Congresses have done before.

In light of the considerable funding uncertainty, states and localities are already pulling back from surface transportation projects. Meanwhile, credit rating agencies are downgrading bonds supported by anticipated federal payments.[19] While complete data is not yet available, a Goldman Sachs analysis found that in previous years when Congress has balked at reauthorizing transportation funding, "uncertainty regarding federal funding has been associated with a temporary slowdown in construction activity, and the slowdown would probably be more severe if payments were actually delayed or reduced."[20] This means that Congress's stalling may have already cost American jobs and slowed down projects.

As suggested above, federal spending on transportation is an important part of our national infrastructure investment, because it traditionally provided a steady and multi-year funding source for major capital projects – especially major road projects that link major economic centers, both regionally and nationally. 44 percent of all surface transportation capital investment comes from federal funds and states with smaller populations tend to rely much more on federal funds.

In 2011, the latest year for which comprehensive data are available for federal, state, and local governments, the U.S. spent more than $215 billion on surface transportation. Taken together, total spending as a share of GDP has been falling, from about 3 percent of GDP in 1962 to only 1.4 percent today. That's more than a 50 percent decline. And although total spending has generally been increasing in real dollar terms since the 1980s, it declined in 2010 and 2011.

As investments have declined, it has become widely recognized by government agencies, state agencies, think tanks, stakeholders, and business groups that our infrastructure is not keeping pace with the demands of a growing economy.

Estimates of the needs for investment vary significantly, as would be expected in any studies of such a large system. In a widely cited report, the American Society of Civil Engineers finds $125 billion per year is needed to maintain and repair our existing surface transportation system, while the National Surface Transportation Infrastructure Financing Commission estimates $139 billion per year (in 2012 dollars). Both estimates are higher than actual capital spending in 2012, which was $103 billion at federal, state, and local government levels.

The Department of Transportation publishes an objective appraisal of the physical conditions, operational performance, and financing mechanisms of highways, bridges, and transit systems based on both their current state and under future investment scenarios. In the most recent Conditions and Performance (C&P) Report, DOT estimates we need $85 to $177 billion.

A strong and efficient infrastructure network is critical to maintaining US competitiveness in a global marketplace. However, in recent years, the United States has fallen considerably behind other advanced countries when it comes to total transportation investment. These investment flows show up in business leader evaluations of the United States as a place to do business. For example, in the World Economic Forum's latest Global Competitive Index, the US ranked 10th for transportation, 18th for roads, and 19th for quality of overall infrastructure—well below other advanced economies. We are well behind countries including Poland, Estonia, Hungary, Spain and Greece.

Business leaders recognize the threats posed to our competitiveness by underinvestment in our infrastructure – a finding backed up by frequent surveys of businesses and employers:

- In 2014, the US Travel Association issued a report finding that 65 percent of travel executives surveyed believe infrastructure is critical to increasing global competitiveness. Moreover, 87 percent believed American Infrastructure was in "fair" or "poor shape", 74 percent said the quality and reliability of the system was important to the success of their business, 76 percent believed the US was not prepared to respond to the competitive demands of increased travel over the next 10 to 15 years, and 96 percent said that that greater investments in maintained and upgrades are needed and that all options should be on the table.

- In 2013, the National Association of Manufacturers surveyed 401 members and found that 70 percent believe American infrastructure is in fair or poor shape and 65 percent do not believe that infrastructure, especially in their region, will be able to respond to the competitive demands of a growing economy over the next 10 to 15 years. It is important to note that the manufacturing sector moves roughly $1.8 trillion (12 percent GDP) of goods and services each year across air, sea, roads, and rail.

- In 2013, The Economist Intelligence Unit took a narrower look by surveying executives from manufacturing companies in the oil and gas, utilities, chemicals and natural resource industries. The EIU found that 87 percent of executives said that aging infrastructure had an impact on their operations in recent years, with 10 percent mentioning that it had caused severe problems in their operations that they were continuing to address.

Conclusion

The data and research presented in this report underscores what the American people already know: investing in infrastructure is essential to the economic health of the nation. That's why poll after poll shows that Americans favor infrastructure investment.

Earlier this year, the President called on Congress to ensure the continuity in surface transportation programs and laid out his vision for a four-year investment plan that would support millions of jobs at home and lay the foundation for American businesses to better compete globally.

Introduced as the GROW AMERICA Act, the proposal would:

- Provide certainty. The multi-year proposal offers states the long term certainty they need to invest in larger, economically transformative projects.

- Increase funding. The President's proposal would provide $302 billion over four years–an increase of 37 percent over current spending levels and creating millions of jobs–to better meet the needs of a growing population and to support a growing economy and growing workforce.
- Make needed reforms. The Administration proposal will create more bang for the buck by streamlining project approval processes, encouraging efficiency and innovation throughout our surface transportation system.

The President has proposed to pay for this critical investment through pro-growth business tax reform. The Administration is eager to work with Congress on tax reform or on other strategies for funding our transportation system. What we can't do is let gridlock in Congress create gridlock across America. It's time to make sure that this important issue gets the attention at home and in Washington that it deserves. This country needs a long-term transportation solution in order to grow the economy, create jobs, and support everyday Americans.

The economic case for investment in our long-term infrastructure is clear— we know it will grow the economy, create good jobs, and position us for long-term growth—and the time for action is now.

Notes

1 Alfred Marshall, *Principles of Economics*, London: Macmillan and Co., Ltd: 1890.

2 David Alan Aschauer, "Is Public Expenditure Productive?" *Journal of Monetary Economics*, 23(2) (March 1989): 177–200.

3 E.g., John G. Fernald, Roads to prosperity? Assessing the link between public capital and productivity, *American Economic Review* 89 (1998): 619–638; Alicia H. Munnell, "Policy Watch: Infrastructure Investment and Economic Growth," *Journal of Economic Perspectives*, 6(4) (Autumn 1992):189–198.

4 E.g., Matthew Kahn and David Levinson, "Fix It First, Expand It Second, Reward It Third: A New Strategy for America's Highways" Hamilton Project, 2011; Edward M. Gramlich, "Infrastructure Investment: A Review Essay," *Journal of Economic Literature*, 32(3) (September 1994): 1176–1196.

5 David Schrank, Bill Eisele, and Tim Lomax, TTI's *2012 Urban Mobility Report*, December 2012.

6 Karen White and Lance R. Grenzeback, "Understanding Freight Bottlenecks," Public Roads 70(5) (March/April 2007). Available at: https://www.fhwa.dot.gov/publications/publicroads/07mar/05.cfm

7 Economic Development Research Group, The Cost of Congestion to the Economy of the Portland Region, 2005, http://www.portofportland.com/PDFPOP/Trade_Trans_Studies_CoCReport1128Final.pdf.

8 Isbell, John, "Maritime and Infrastructure Impact on Nike's Inbound Delivery Supply Chain," TRB Freight Roundtable, 2006, http://www.trb.org/conferences/FDM/Isbell.pdf.

9 Bowe, John. 2006. "The High Cost of Congestion" Presentation to the TRB Freight Roundtable, October 24, www.trb.org/conferences/FDM/Bowe.pdf.

10 Andrew F. Haughwout, "Public infrastructure investments, productivity and welfare in fixed geographic areas " Journal of Public Economics (March 2002) 83(3): 405-428.
11 Weinstein, B. et al. "The Initial Economic Impacts of the DART LRT System." Center for Economic Development and Research, University of North Texas, 1999.
12 Garrett, T. "Light Rail Transit in America: Policy Issues and Prospects for Economic Development," Federal Reserve Bank of St. Louis, 2004.
13 Gruen, A."The Effect of CTA and METRA Stations on Residential Property Values." Regional Transportation Authority, 1997
14 Landis, J. et al. "Rail Transit Investments, Real Estate Values, and Land Use Change: A Comparative Analysis of Five California Rail Systems." Institute of Urban and Regional Development, UC Berkeley, 1995.
15 Cervero, R. et al. "Land Value Impacts of Rail Transit Services in San Diego County," Urban Land Institute, 2002.

16 Lucy Dadayan and Donald J. Boyd, "April 'Surprises' More Surprising Than Expected: Depressed Income Tax Collections Adding to Budget Pressures," Rockefeller Institute of Government Special Report, June 2014.

17 James R. Hines, Hilary Hoynes, and Alan Krueger, "Another Look at Whether a Rising Tide Lifts All Boats," in The Roaring '90s: Can Full Employment Be Sustained?, edited by Alan B. Krueger and Robert Solow, Russell Sage and Century Fund, 2001

18 Currie, Janet, and Reed Walker. 2011. "Traffic Congestion and Infant Health: Evidence from E-ZPass." American Economic Journal: Applied Economic Journal: Applied Economics, 3(1): 65-90.

19 Jim Watts, "Moody's Lowers GARVEES as HTF Evaporates," Bond Buyer, June 18, 2014

20 Goldman Sachs Global Macro Research, "US Daily: Congress Finally Begins to Make Progress on Infrastructure Spending" July 9, 2014.

5

Will Contamination of Water by Lead Pipes Be Stopped?

Julia Franz

Julia Franz is a freelance writer for Public Radio International *and an assistant producer at* Minnesota Public Radio News.

Julia Franz focuses on the problem of lead pipe usage in the US water system. The case of lead contamination in the drinking water of Flint, Michigan, is well known, and its causes have been well reported by news media. This viewpoint reports on how other cities are grappling with the problem and provides suggestions for homeowners, pointing to the challenges and limitations faced by public infrastructure. It also indicates that large-scale initiatives to repair and replace aging infrastructure are favorable to temporary solutions that require lower investment.

I n 2014, the city of Flint, Michigan changed the source of its water from the city of Detroit to the Flint River. But in the transition to river water, officials didn't implement proper anti-corrosion measures. Lead leached from old pipes into the water supply, and in some homes, lead levels measured 10 times higher than the limit set by the Environmental Protection Agency.

Last month, lead levels in Flint's city water finally tested below federal-action level. But residents are still being cautioned to use filters on their faucets, or to drink bottled water.

Flint's current water infrastructure has been damaged by corrosion, experts say. And the ongoing cleanup in Flint holds lessons for other American communities, many of which still have old lead pipes in their underground networks.

"We once thought we could do a very good job protecting the public and make the water safe even if they have a lead pipe," says Marc Edwards, an engineer at Virginia Tech who alerted officials to high lead levels in Flint's water.

"And in the aftermath of Flint, what we now realize, is, that's not the case, that probably we're never going to be able to say that it's safe to drink water from a lead pipe — not only in Flint but in fact, all around the United States."

In Flint's case, officials decided against adding a corrosion inhibitor when they first switched to river water. As Edwards explains, the decision not to use the chemical, which coats pipes to keep lead out of the water supply, had lasting consequences.

"There is damage that was done during this time period that's irreversible," he says. "Specifically, corrosion eats holes in metals, it weakens the pipes. So, to some extent, during this time there were massive outbreaks of water main breaks. Literally, the water was eating holes through the iron pipes."

Edwards calls corrosion control "an important Band-Aid," but says that ultimately, it doesn't solve the problem of lead in public water systems. That takes replacing the pipes — including the galvanized iron ones that have been tainted by lead.

"What we discovered in Flint is that some of the worst houses actually had a lead pipe followed by a galvanized iron pipe," he explains. "And what had happened over the almost a century some of these pipes had been in the ground is, the iron rust on the galvanized iron pipe sponged up lead at very, very high levels. And when the corrosion control was discontinued, that iron rust fell off with a lot of lead coming with it."

As of January, Flint had removed about 800 lead-tainted pipes. The city estimates as many as 28,000 more may need to be replaced.

But in Flint, locating lead pipes hasn't meant a one-stop look at a service map. Flint's not alone. Lindsey Smith of Michigan Public Radio has reported that many cities don't know where their lead pipes are buried — but an estimated 6 million lead service lines are still in use across the US. "They're really common in older cities," she says.

After Flint's crisis began, Martin Kaufman, an environmental hydrologist at the University of Michigan in Flint, helped the city digitally piece together information about where its lead service lines are. He says it wasn't easy — Flint's records were all on paper.

"The city of Flint had used paper maps to record an indicator on parcel maps, 240 of them, what type of pipe was servicing a parcel in the city," he says. And the data, which was only recorded until 1984, was also incomplete. Records were missing for 11,000 property parcels — nearly one-fifth of the 56,000 total parcels in Flint.

Kaufman says it was enough to create a "preliminary indication" of where the city's lead service pipes were. But other cities have begun the process of replacing lead pipes, only to discover a much bigger problem than they'd imagined.

Washington, DC, for instance, tried to replace its lead pipes in the early 2000s. "And the more they looked, the more lead pipes they found," Edwards says. The city ran into another problem: Many residents weren't willing to pay for their share of the new lines connecting their homes to the water main.

"Less than 1 percent of the people did that," he says. According to The Washington Post, the city performed nearly 15,000 partial replacements between 2004 and 2008, replacing lead lines until they reached private property. "And so this is actually creating a long-term problem in that the city's records indicate there's no lead pipe," Edwards adds. "You've also disturbed the lead pipe and you've connected it to copper, and actually you've left the situation worse than you found it, in many cases."

Eventually, he says, Washington, DC "spent $100 million, actually increased the incidence of lead poisoning, and found more lead pipes than they'd ever imagine. And they just gave up."

Meanwhile, cities like Madison, Wisconsin, and Lansing, Michigan, have successfully removed their lead service lines. Edwards notes that in Lansing, the city owned the entire water line leading to homes. "That was one advantage they had to getting all of their lead pipes out of the ground."

And according to Smith, other cities like Kalamazoo, Michigan, are testing for lead more stringently than before. "They're actually verifying that they are testing the homes that they're supposed to," she says. That means sending people into homes to physically check water lines, rather than basing information on records or dates of construction.

"And that is such a key because I mean, in Detroit's case, as an example, I mean that's the biggest city in Michigan, and it has, by far, the most lead service lines of any city in the state," she says. "And they were determining where lead service lines were based on the year that the home was built, or the year that the home had attached to the water main."

For anyone concerned about lead pipes in their city or home, Edwards says to check online for tips on identifying pipe materials. "The one thing you can be sure of if you have a lead pipe coming into your house, you have a very significant health risk," he says.

"What you can't be sure of, is, if you have a copper or galvanized iron pipe coming into your house, that there's a lead pipe somewhere out there that you don't see. And so for that, you need the city to come and usually dig a hole in your yard, unfortunately."

And for immediate protection, Edwards recommends that consumers worried about lead install a filter on their faucet.

"It cleans the water that passes through all the lead pipes, and there's no chance that the water will get contaminated after it flows from the faucet into your cup or cooking utensil."

6

How Many Bridges Will Collapse Before the Infrastructure Is Repaired?

Dave Schaper

Dave Schaper is a Chicago based National Desk reporter for National Public Radio. Schaper covers news in Chicago and around the Midwest.

The 2017 bridge collapse in Minneapolis was well publicized by the media. In this viewpoint, Dave Schaper recounts details of the collapse and statistics on bridge safety from the National Transportation Safety Board. Schaper also reports on the progress made in Minnesota to fix other bridges and reveals a startling statistic: that throughout the US over 55,000 bridges are in serious need of repair. Unless other states follow Minnesota's lead and prioritize bridge and road improvements—as many states already have—more catastrophic incidents are almost certain to occur.

Ten years ago, the Interstate 35W bridge over the Mississippi River in downtown Minneapolis collapsed, sending cars, trucks and even a school bus that were crawling over it in bumper-to-bumper rush hour traffic plummeting into the river below and onto the rocky shore.

Thirteen people were killed, 145 more were injured, many of them seriously.

The bridge collapse sparked immediate calls in Minnesota and across the country invest big in repairing and replacing the nation's aging and crumbling infrastructure.

A decade later, experts say there have been some improvements, but there are still tens of thousands of bridges nationwide that need to be fixed or replaced.

In the immediate aftermath of the 35W bridge collapse, the Minnesota Department of Transportation came under intense scrutiny. The interstate highway bridge had been classified as structurally deficient, meaning that it was aging and in need of repair. In fact, some repair work was going on when it fell. And the bridge was also rated as fracture critical, meaning the failure of just one vital component could cause the whole bridge to collapse.

But in fact, neither of those classifications means a bridge is necessarily dangerous. And the National Transportation Safety Board determined that it was a design flaw, and not deferred maintenance, neglect, or other problems, that caused the 35W bridge to collapse. Gusset plates that hold the bridge's huge steel beams together were only half as thick as they should have been. The NTSB also found that nearly 300 tons of construction equipment and materials stockpiled on the bridge deck for the ongoing repair work contributed to the collapse by further stressing the crucial gusset plate that failed.

Nancy Daubenberger was still in the bridge office of the MnDOT just after 6:00 p.m. CT, when a colleague called with the horrifying and heartbreaking news.

"The first feeling was shock," says Daubenberger, then a bridge engineer for the state and now the director of engineering services for MnDOT. "The shock that came over me, that such a large bridge like that could collapse ... it was devastating and tragic and shocking; a very, very sad situation."

Daubenberger says the state immediately inspected gusset plates on every single truss bridge in the state to ensure that they were safe, and within months of the collapse, the Minnesota state legislature raised the gas tax and funded a $2.5 billion bridge improvement program.

"The bill established a program to have all structurally deficient bridges and fracture critical bridges repaired or replaced within 10 years, so by June 30, 2018," says Daubenberger.

The I-35W bridge was rebuilt within 14 months.

Daubenberger says 172 Minnesota bridges were identified as structurally deficient or fracture critical. About 35 of them were determined to need only routine, preventative maintenance. About 120 of them have been repaired or replaced, while the 18 remaining bridges are either under construction now and/or are on track to be repaired or replaced before next summer's deadline.

"I'm very proud of our accomplishments since 2008," says Daubenberger. "Unfortunately, it was a very tragic situation ... and we never want ever happen again and we're doing a lot of things differently now to ensure that sort of thing doesn't happen."

Minnesota has also stepped up and improved bridge inspections, and now even uses drones sometimes to take photos and video of spots on bridges that are difficult for human inspectors to reach.

The state now gets outside independent peer reviews of bridge design plans, and it's revamped its bridge maintenance worker training program.

"Certainly we've done a lot to ensure the safety of bridges so it doesn't happen again, so I feel confident about the advancements we've made in bridge design, construction, inspection, maintenance and that all works towards good bridge safety," Daubenberger says.

But while Minnesota has acted aggressively to reduce it's number of structurally deficient bridges, what about the rest of the country?

"America's infrastructure is like a third-world country," says former Republican Rep. Ray LaHood, who served as transportation secretary under President Obama.

The American Road and Transportation Builders Association, which tracks the number of bridges with structural defects in each state, found 55,710 bridges nationwide that need to be repaired or replaced.

"That's a very costly item," says LaHood, adding that "most states simply do not have the money to take care of them, so they're patching them and they're doing the best they can to keep them in a state of repair where people can drive over them, but it's a serious, serious problem."

Federal funding for bridges and other infrastructure needs has remained flat over the past decade, and LaHood is critical of Congress and his own party in particular, for not raising the gasoline tax to increase spending to repair and replace bridges and address other dire infrastructure needs.

President Trump has promised to invest a trillion dollars on improving the nation's infrastructure, but other than a broad and vague outline of priorities and talk of leveraging private investment for projects, he has yet to unveil a plan.

With federal revenue lagging, many states have followed Minnesota's lead and increased their own gas taxes to fund bridge and road improvements. In the last four years, 26 states have raised gasoline taxes, including red states dominated by fiscal conservatives. That includes Indiana, Tennessee, South Carolina, West Virginia and Montana this year alone.

And state funding efforts, combined with a greater emphasis on bridge needs since the collapse, appear to be helping improve bridge conditions.

According to the American Society of Civil Engineers, 12 percent of the nation's bridges were rated as structurally deficient in 2007, but only 9 percent are in that category today.

Still, ARTBA, the builders' association, estimates it would take more than three decades to repair or replace all those more than 55,000 bridges that need it. It's a challenge that will no doubt grow as structures age and federal interest continues to lag.

7

Overall, Infrastructure Is Not Crumbling

Jeffrey Harding

Jeffrey Harding is an adjunct professor at Santa Barbara City College, and a real estate investor. He writes about economics and finance.

Jeffrey Harding argues that on a large scale infrastructure is not crumbling. Harding admits that while some aspects of American infrastructure are in bad shape and that specific regions around the United States have problems, the majority of American infrastructure is acceptable and consistently improving in quality. Harding cites studies to back up his claims and further analyzes suggestions made by current President Donald Trump to determine their potential impacts.

Every year the American Society of Civil Engineers (ASCE) comes out with a report card on the condition of America's infrastructure. We got a D+ this year. According to them, "Deteriorating infrastructure is impeding our ability to compete in the thriving global economy, and improvements are necessary to ensure our country is built for the future."

They calculate that every family in America will lose $3,400 a year because of infrastructure deficiencies. If the problem isn't fixed, they say, GDP will lose $4 trillion a year by then (2025) and 2.5 million jobs will be lost. They recommend an additional

"Our Roads Are Crumbling and Other Infrastructure Myths," by Jeffrey Harding, Foundation for Economic Education, July 17, 2017. https://fee.org/articles/our-roads-are-crumbling-and-other-infrastructure-myths/. Licensed under CC BY 4.0.

$1.1 trillion of spending on transportation (roads and bridges) over the next 10 years to correct this problem.

President Donald Trump says that we need to spend $1 trillion to "transform America's crumbling infrastructure into a golden opportunity for accelerated economic growth and more rapid productivity gains."

Liberals and conservatives alike get teary-eyed when they hear this. They think that massive spending, especially on roads and bridges, will "put people back to work" and make America more productive.

Here is the reality: America's infrastructure is not crumbling, massive spending won't create any permanent jobs, and productivity is not suffering because of our infrastructure. These are economic myths that lobbyists, infrastructure contractors, and the ASCE perpetuate to get fat contracts.

Things Just Keep Getting Better

Let me back up for a moment and say that, yes, our transportation system, for example, is an important factor in productivity and inefficiencies could harm productivity. Los Angeles is a glaring example of inefficiency since it again was the world's worst metro area for traffic congestion (104 hours per year wasted in traffic; NYC – 89; SF – 83). Surely commuters' time would be better spent in more productive activities than listening to NPR.

Let me also note that by "we" as in "we need to spend $X trillion ...", the "we" are your local, state, and federal governments who own and operate our roads and bridges. They are the reason we have transportation infrastructure problems. You have only to look to your politicians to place the blame.

When the ASCE comes out with their Report Card every year, our news media dutifully start their reporting by showing a bridge or road somewhere that is crumbling and it is cited as an exemplar of the problem of "our crumbling infrastructure." What they don't tell you is that if you look at transportation issues over time, things have been getting better, not worse (except the aforementioned traffic congestion).

The Reason Foundation's studies on state-owned highways (they are widely recognized as being leaders in this field) and other studies on highways and bridges reveal that there have been significant improvements of infrastructure measures like road and bridge quality and fatalities over the past 20 or 30 years. The facts are that, on the state level, overall spending on highways doubled during that period, and overall measures of highway transportation have improved.

They also found there was not a good correlation on a state by state basis of spending to improvements – in some states spending resulted in improvements, in others, not. They also say that problem areas are usually concentrated in a few states, such as California and New York's congestion.

So, some infrastructure is "crumbling", but the overall trend is that it isn't. Most of the noise is from those who would benefit from infrastructure spending and the politicians who enjoy ribbon-cutting.

Creating Jobs

The idea that massive government spending on infrastructure will create jobs is another myth. If you recall the $787 billion 2009 American Recovery and Reinvestment Act (ARRA), the Obama Administration told us that such fiscal stimulus would create jobs and promote economic recovery. There is simply no credible evidence that such Keynesian stimulus did anything to help economic recovery.

Curve-fitting estimates at the time by the bill's proponents were wildly incorrect. The $100 billion or so of ARRA that was spent on "infrastructure" had no impact at all on the economy and those "jobs" came and went along with the wasteful spending. ARRA did not produce anything but massive budget deficits and more debt while the economy stagnated.

President Trump campaigned on a dark vision of America that the economy was in shambles, along with our infrastructure, that he would fix it, create jobs, and revive the economy.

The facts suggest the opposite of his campaign rhetoric.

Presently the economy is considered to be at full employment with unemployment at its lowest rate since 2001. One could argue that there is little slack in labor supply. Thus, if the goal of infrastructure spending advocates is to boost employment, that is unnecessary.

If the goal is to boost America's productivity, then one needs to ask if massive infrastructure spending would accomplish that. As I have pointed out, the state of our transportation system is not crumbling, and in fact has been improving over the years. That is not to say that some states or counties don't need upgrades, but they are in the minority.

If the ASCE's assumption that poor infrastructure is impeding progress, then we should look at the LA metropolitan area where traffic congestion is the worst in the world to see if they are correct. Based on their logic, LA's economy should be suffering. But it is not. In fact, if you compare LA's GDP to the rise in total US GDP, LA's upward trend is almost identical if not rising even faster.

Public-Private Partnerships

What the proponents of massive infrastructure spending fail to understand is that productivity is based mostly on private capital spending on more efficient means of production, distribution, and sales: new factories, new machinery, new software to improve production and logistics, new methods of sales, and so on. These are the primary causes of economic growth. For example, the "crumbling infrastructure" seems to have done little to impede the efficiencies created by the "just-in-time" supply chain that relies on quick transportation.

While many of the Trump Administration's populist themes will do much to harm the economy, their proposal on infrastructure has some merit if done properly. We can forget their claims of economic transformation, but we should be thinking about better ways to handle infrastructure projects. This is why we need public-private partnerships (P3).

P3s let private companies design, build, and operate new infrastructure projects. According to Bob Poole, the Reason Foundation's expert on privatization, P3s will result in projects that will be more economically productive (no bridges to nowhere) and would be much more cost effective.

Remarkably, the Trump Administration is proposing P3s to accomplish future infrastructure spending. The Trump proposal relies on tax credits for P3 projects, not $1 trillion in new spending. These projects would be based on privatized systems which generate an income stream, and are financed by revenue bonds. Thus, the risks of these projects are shifted to private companies rather than to taxpayers.

The Trump P3 proposal has many "ifs" in it to result in an effective program. But, if these hurdles can be overcome, then, as Poole says, "this election has opened the door to major changes in what the federal government does and how it goes about it. ... My guess is that these changes will be very positive for P3 infrastructure."

Remember, "if it weren't for the government, who would neglect the roads?"

8

Latin America Must Modernize Its Infrastructure

Marisol Argueta de Barillas

Marisol Argueta de Barillas publishes articles on international affairs as an executive committee member of the World Economic Forum and head of Latin American regional agenda.

The United States isn't the only country facing the challenges of updating infrastructure: Marisol Argueta de Barillas points out that countries throughout Latin America are also working to modernize their infrastructure. Barillas discusses Panama City as a model of Latin American infrastructure: it is a city rich in Latin American culture, and at the same time it has successfully invested and developed its infrastructure, suggesting that modernization does not have to mean uniformity in cities. Barillas maintains that the rest of Latin America should model development after the success of Panama.

Next month, several hundred leaders from every different sector of society will arrive in Panama City for the ninth World Economic Forum on Latin America. It is an appropriate setting for a meeting focused on Latin America's opportunity to leap forward in terms of growth, productivity and infrastructure development.

Panama City has a traditional Latin American flavour, with its historic and colourful colonial centre. It also embodies the

"The three big issues facing Latin America," by Marisol Argueta de Barillas, World Economic Forum, March 26, 2014. Reprinted by permission.

dynamic economic growth of the region with a skyline to rival that of any major trading hub. Located at the heart of the Americas, it is well connected and will, this year, celebrate the centenary of the Panama Canal.

The country as a whole has strived tremendously in the area of competitiveness. With extensive investment in infrastructure, it has created innovative business models to attract international companies. As a result, Panama has developed a thriving economy based mainly on services, with very high, sustained rates of growth for the past 10 years.

It is from this perspective that we will focus on Latin America's efforts to drive economic dynamism, innovate for social inclusion and environmental sustainability, and modernize its economic and institutional infrastructure.

Latin America has vast natural resources and important human capital. It has shown its financial resilience with sustained economic growth for the past decade, and despite complex economic perspectives, it is now open for greater investment in a host of different industries.

In Brazil, for example, the Logistics Investment Programme, a US$ 121 billion government-led infrastructure investment portfolio, is based on strategic partnerships with the private sector, and in Mexico, a wide-ranging package of reforms to labour laws, education and strategic economic sectors, has opened up great opportunities in the energy, communications and manufacturing industries. This is an inspiring model that could be used in other countries, both in and outside the region.

But it is important to tackle remaining structural challenges. Latin American countries must diversify their drivers of growth. Commodities exports represented 60% of the region's exports compared with 40%, ten years ago. More than the expansion of its volume, many have benefited from high commodities prices, but this is a volatile base for an economy, as demand has faltered, particularly from China, because of the global economic slowdown. It has also implied the substitution of locally manufactured goods by imports, affecting the region's manufacturing capacity and competitiveness, in some cases. This opens a timely opportunity for the adoption of new regional industrial policies to promote enhanced specialization based on knowledge, increased value added and improved value chains that also incorporate SMEs. To this end, economic integration initiatives like the Pacific Alliance are positive examples of political will towards the achievement of more efficient flows of goods and services, simplified customs procedures and reduced red tape, in general.

From a competitiveness perspective, the region must modernise its infrastructure and logistics, and reduce the transportation costs, or risk impeding further productivity and development. This aspect is crucial and requires focused attention. Physical infrastructure is, of course, key and its modernization requires sufficient financial resources, that could, in some cases, require innovative public and private investment models or fresh resources and increased revenue from fiscal reform, together with strong institutions to monitor public spending.

But we are also referring to technological and institutional infrastructure, which enables businesses to commit to a region and gives investors the certainty they require for the long term. Latin America must bring in new technologies and develop enhanced public policy and innovative business models, if it is to transcend the status quo and develop a more advanced economy.

Another serious concern is the degree of inequality in the region. It is true there have been impressive positive outcomes from poverty alleviation programmes, which have allowed for the emergence of a larger middle class and has created models for worldwide practice. But much progress still needs to be made in terms of equal opportunities, gender parity and inclusive growth. The meeting next month will include sessions to address the need to invest in human capital and improve the quality of education and skills for the long-term development of the region, as well as the need to respond to the demands of its growing middle class, including efficient and better public services and more high-quality employments.

The issue of public insecurity and drug trafficking is also important. We will have a session looking at innovative and collaborative solutions, not just in terms of law enforcement but also in areas of crime prevention, rehabilitation and social reinsertion.

Among the more than 600 participants at the meeting, there will be eight heads of state, more than 60 government ministers and public officials from almost every country in Latin America, and some from outside the region. All the heads of the regional and hemispheric organisations will attend, as will business and thought leaders from Latin America and around the world.

At the same time, Panama City will host the first gathering of Global Shapers – young leaders – between the ages of 20 and 30 years old – from every country in Latin America and the Caribbean. It is particularly exciting to have young, energetic voices providing their views on how they would like to see the region develop.

Our aim is that these leaders will emerge from the meeting inspired and willing to use what they have learned from the multi-stakeholder dialogues in their realm of impact and influence. That is how we will open pathways for continued shared progress in Latin America.

9

Bipartisan Bickering Stalls Infrastructure Improvements

Heidi Crebo-Rediker

Heidi Crebo-Rediker is an adjunct senior fellow at the Council on Foreign Relations. Crebo-Rediker is an expert on matters of infrastructure, international finance, economic policy, and women and economic growth.

In the following viewpoint, Heidi Crebo-Rediker reiterates remarks made by President Trump in his 2018 State of the Union address and his call for improved infrastructure. Democrats and Republicans agree with this basic request, but action is stalled nonetheless due to disagreement about how the plan should be implemented. Crebo-Rediker analyzes and details the difficulties that are stalling the President's call for action.

A bipartisan deal on infrastructure seems doable—but with the devil in the details, it is much harder than it looks.

As expected, President Trump used his State of the Union speech to highlight his appeal for bipartisan support for his $1.5 trillion plan to "rebuild our crumbling infrastructure...to give us safe, fast, reliable and modern infrastructure that our economy needs and our people deserve." Bravo. The need to address this country's infrastructure deficiencies is one area where there is real bipartisan agreement. Unfortunately, once you get past the top line agreement that something must be done, the devilish details emerge and fundamental disagreements become clear.

Sadly, in spite of a cooperative outreach on infrastructure, a bipartisan deal in 2018 appears unlikely. There are huge gaps between how Democrats and Republicans approach everything from how to use federal dollars, where to use federal dollars, how many of those federal dollars should be used, and where to find them. Battles over infrastructure are not likely to be limited to Democrats versus Republicans. One of the reasons that infrastructure is so difficult is because it also pits the federal government against state and local governments, which are being asked to shoulder an increasingly disproportionate share of the burden, and rural against urban, making a comprehensive solution that much more politically and financially divisive.

On the back of Trump's speech, and the delayed, detailed White House infrastructure plan to be released soon, I expect that we will be hearing a lot about infrastructure in the coming months.[1] Headlines around big ticket proposals from both parties, as well as Congressional hearings and the likely introduction of a variety of infrastructure bills, will raise expectations of a bipartisan deal, especially given strong popular support.[2]

Yet, a bipartisan deal on infrastructure in 2018 remains deeply challenging. There are wide ideological differences between Republicans and Democrats, and no mutually agreeable plan on how to pay for the underlying $200 billion appropriation that was floated in the early preview of the White House plan last May. Republicans who turned a blind eye to increased deficits in the context of tax reform are likely to regain their sight and renew focus on deficit control when it comes to spending on infrastructure. Repatriation, once considered a potential "pay for" for infrastructure, was already used to "pay for" tax reform. There is no obvious way to pay for any package.

There are also fundamental differences between Democratic and Republican approaches on how and where to invest federal dollars. The White House approach is mainly through private sector and non-federal funding of investment and the Democrats want mainly a public sector approach. Given that the Trump administration's private sector approach would disadvantage rural communities as contrasted with more commercially viable higher density urban areas, there is likely to be a strong dividing line on this issue between rural and urban districts regardless of political party affiliation.

The administration's increased burden on state and local governments will also prove divisive. States already provide the majority of US infrastructure investment through their own municipal bond issuance. Likewise, some states are better prepared than others to both *evaluate* and *utilize* innovative financing arrangements with more significant private sector involvement. Not all state and local governments have technical expertise to evaluate the costs and benefits of private investment alternatives, and in some cases there is still no state legislation to govern private infrastructure investment. Finally, if criteria for obtaining federal funds rest too heavily on a state's ability to attract non-federal funds, government funding could end up targeting profitable infrastructure projects, and leave critical unprofitable projects on the wayside.

While President Trump can use the pulpit of the State of the Union to propose bipartisan cooperation on infrastructure and provide the starting gun, it is Congress that will ultimately need to play the leading role in making any infrastructure package a reality. Given wide gaps between rhetoric and the reality of finding a way to pay for proposed infrastructure plans that could pass both houses, including the need for support from at least nine Democratic senators, real progress on a sorely needed infrastructure package in 2018 might advance the ball, but reaching the goal line will remain elusive.

The most hopeful signs we are likely to see this year would be movement towards a bipartisan approach to how to pay for whatever compromises lie ahead. But even then, the road ahead is bumpy. Unless Democrats and Republicans can also agree on the details of how and where to invest precious federal funds, big and bold infrastructure investment may, unfortunately, remain a future initiative rather than a reality during the Trump administration. Calls for bipartisan cooperation on infrastructure are easy. Infrastructure, however, is hard.

Notes

[1] Building on the administration's brief overview released last May and possibly reflecting the leaked White House draft infrastructure plan from last week.

[2] The Democrats also laid out their own $1 trillion infrastructure plan and consider infrastructure investment to be one of their key policy issues.

10

Multiple Factors Influence Infrastructure Improvement

Douglas C. Smith and Kevin L. Kliesen

Douglas C. Smith is a research analyst at the Federal Reserve Bank of St. Louis, where Kevin L. Kliesen is a business economist and research officer.

Douglas C. Smith and Kevin L. Kliesen analyze the issue of infrastructure from an economic perspective. First, they assert that the United States' infrastructure is in need of repair, citing the surveys done by the American Society of Civil Engineers (ASCE) as evidence. The authors then detail factors that affect the situation, including budgetary and governmental issues, along with the trends in infrastructure spending. They assert that a careful understanding of the state of modern infrastructure is necessary for effective planning going forward.

The nation's public infrastructure is crumbling and in dire need of repair, according to conventional wisdom. This view seems to have become more strident after the Minneapolis bridge collapse in 2007. The American Recovery and Reinvestment Act of 2009 (ARRA) ostensibly addresses this concern by providing $111 billion for infrastructure and science projects. Of this amount, about a quarter ($27.5 billion) was set aside for spending on highway construction. Officials in the seven states that comprise parts or

"Digging Into the Infrastructure Debate," by Douglas C. Smith, Kevin L. Kliesen, Federal Reserve Bank of St. Louis, July, 2009. Reprinted by permission.

all of the Eighth Federal Reserve District have already proposed infrastructure projects totaling several billion dollars.

A well-functioning public infrastructure system is necessary to support rising living standards over time, but other factors are also crucial to improving these standards. Moreover, the evidence that the nation's public infrastructure has fallen into wide-spread disrepair does not appear to be overwhelming. Even if it turns out to be, ongoing and emerging structural changes in the economy may necessitate a more careful assessment of future outlays for traditional infrastructure.

The State of Public Infrastructure

The nation's infrastructure can be thought of as its tangible capital stock (income-earning assets), whether owned by private companies or the government.[1] This can include everything from the Toyota manufacturing plant in Indiana to the FedEx and UPS warehousing and distribution facilities in Memphis and Louisville, respectively.

However, to most people, infrastructure is the nation's streets, highways, bridges and other structures that are typically owned and operated by the government. More than 75 percent of the government's capital stock is owned by state and local governments.

Several recent reports on the health of the nation's infrastructure rate it to be in relatively poor shape. According to some organizations, such as the American Society of Civil Engineers (ASCE), this is a long-standing concern. Every few years, the society rates 15 categories of public infrastructure. In its 2009 Report Card for America's Infrastructure, the ASCE said that only three of 15 categories merited a C (mediocre), while the remaining 12 barely passed with a D (poor). This year's cumulative grade (D) is unchanged from the society's previous report in 2005, and it differs little from the reports issued in 2001 (D+) and in 1998 (D). The ASCE further says that the United States needs to more than double planned infrastructure spending over the next five years, or by about $1.1 trillion, to put the nation's infrastructure in "good condition." About half of this infrastructure gap is due to deteriorating roads and bridges.

Citing the ASCE's findings, the National Governors Association (NGA) published *An Infrastructure Vision for the 21st Century* this year.[2] According to the NGA, "The nation's infrastructure system is no longer adequately meeting the nation's needs and faces several long-term challenges that affect our ability to maintain and enhance our competitiveness, quality of life and environmental sustainability."

Other studies sound similar alarms. For example, the Organisation for Economic Cooperation and Development (OECD) said in 2007 that advanced countries besides the United States face similar problems:

"A gap is opening up in OECD countries between the infrastructure investments required for the future, and the capacity of the public sector to meet those requirements from traditional sources." [3]

Yet, the Congressional Budget Office estimated last year that spending on the U.S. transportation infrastructure was roughly $16 billion below the spending needed to maintain current levels of service.

Divergent studies about infrastructure gaps are not new. In a comprehensive study published in 1994, the late economist (and former Fed governor) Edward Gramlich noted that engineering assessments of infrastructure gaps that were originally published in the early 1980s became progressively smaller over time "as they were done more carefully." Of course, it is certainly possible that engineering assessments have improved over time in response to these criticisms.

Increased traffic congestion is one of the costs associated with inadequate public spending on infrastructure. In a 2007 report, the Texas Transportation Institute at Texas A&M University estimated that the costs associated with travel delays and wasted fuel (congestion costs) in nearly 450 urban areas totaled $710 per person (in 2005 dollars), about 25 percent higher in inflation-adjusted terms from a decade earlier.[4] Since a significant portion of these congestion costs reflects the fact that a scarce resource (roads) is made freely available to everyone early in the morning and late in the afternoon (rush hour traffic), economists generally argue that some form of congestion pricing—rather than new infrastructure outlays—would mitigate these costs.[5]

The Economics of Infrastructure Spending

Economics is the study of how society responds to incentives when deciding how to allocate scarce resources. Since this decision process necessarily involves trade-offs, economies that prosper over time tend to allocate their economic resources to the purchase of capital that produces the highest rate of return. In the private sphere, this generally occurs as businesses strive to maximize profits and returns to shareholders. In the public sphere, these questions are equally valid, but answering them often requires information that is not readily available. For example, how does a city determine the rate of return on a new police station, unless it can accurately determine the value of future crimes that might be prevented?

Competing demands for public services besides infrastructure compound the problem confronting government authorities. For example, if a city has $X to spend on infrastructure improvements, will the rate of return on a highway overpass produce a higher rate of return than an improvement to a city's sewer or flood-control systems?

These questions are often difficult to answer, but are nonetheless important. Some might believe that the presence of trade-offs forces government officials to neglect bridges and other facilities. However, the rhetoric is sometimes not matched by the reality.

Most economists believe that capital formation is an important determinant of economic growth over time because more capital per worker usually leads to a higher level of output per worker (productivity). In the late 1980s and the early 1990s, many academic articles were written that discussed the effects of public infrastructure on the nation's productivity. In particular, some economists suggested that a reduction in public capital spending may have been an important contributor to the 1973 slowdown in U.S. labor productivity growth.[6]

Although other factors were likely more important in explaining the productivity slowdown, public infrastructure is nevertheless important because it facilitates the production of many private goods and services. For example, many trucking firms and package delivery services are heavy users of the nation's streets, highways and public airports. Accordingly, additions to the public capital stock can improve living standards, as well as provide other benefits not captured in the economic statistics, such as time saving or outdoor recreation.

Over time, additions or subtractions to the capital stock will depend on both macroeconomic factors (how well or poorly the economy is performing) and microeconomic factors (performance of the state or local economy or the ability of state and local authorities to raise money). Some of the key macroeconomic determinants of infrastructure spending include:[7]

1. Growth of Per Capita Income and Technical Change
The development of the internal combustion engine and commercial aviation has dramatically altered the scope and composition of the nation's infrastructure. For example, as the U.S. grew wealthier after World War II, the number of registered vehicles per person age 16 and older doubled between 1948 (0.4) and 1971 (0.81). One of the responses to this development was the interstate highway system.

2. Population Change
Having more people generally entails a larger demand for public schools, hospitals, fire stations and other basic infrastructure.

3. Other Factors, Such As the Relative Cost of Public Services

Increases in commodity and energy prices have significantly increased construction costs since 2002. Higher construction costs generally mean fewer bridge or street projects.

The Government's Role in Infrastructure Spending

Economists have long argued that the provision of certain kinds of infrastructure is one of the major responsibilities of government. In fact, Adam Smith in *The Wealth of Nations* argued that providing public works is the "third and last duty" of the government.[8] In a market economy, new goods and services naturally occur in response to perceived profit opportunities. For example, if a firm correctly perceives an unmet demand for a shopping center, it will reap considerable profits from its construction.

However, this is generally different for public goods like highways or bridges. First, public goods are usually very expensive to build and maintain, and the state or local government generally reaps no profit from its use by the citizenry. If a bridge is designed and built to generate revenue for the governing authority, it would have to impose a toll sufficiently high enough to cover its construction costs, maintenance and opportunity cost. However, if the toll is too high, drivers may use an alternative route, leaving revenue lower than expected. Regardless, the new bridge would probably still reduce traffic and congestion in other areas, which means that there would be benefits accruing to those who did not use the bridge.

Public goods that provide social benefits to those who do not directly use the bridge are called externalities. The presence of externalities means that a private firm would not be willing to finance such a large capital outlay unless it can earn a profit—in other words, capturing a part of the revenue generated by using the bridge (in our example). This is why most large-scale capital projects are funded by the taxpayer—even if some taxpayers who do not use the bridge benefit from its construction.

At the state and local (microeconomic) level, there are many additional factors that will influence an authority's decision to increase or rebuild its infrastructure. These include political considerations, engineering assessments and the performance of the local economy (which affects tax revenue). Other microeconomic determinants include:

1. Budget Constraints
Most state and local governments have some form of a balanced budget requirement, which limits their ability to fund expensive new projects out of general revenue. When revenue declines, as in recessions, public projects often get canceled or delayed.

2. Net Benefits
A project will be economically feasible if its benefits exceed its costs. Although estimating budgetary costs are straightforward, there may be nonbudgetary costs—for example, excessive reliance on debt may reduce a state's or municipality's credit rating, forcing it to pay a higher rate of interest. Estimating the dollar value of benefits can be extremely difficult.

3. Rate of Return
A project is also economically feasible if its real rate of return exceeds an estimated real interest rate that could be earned on revenue invested elsewhere (opportunity cost). According to Gramlich, estimates of the real rate of return on public infrastructure vary greatly—ranging from large and positive (maintaining current highway conditions) to negative (reinforcing structures to exceed minimum standards).

Trends in Infrastructure Spending
As the nation's policymakers debate the size and scope of future infrastructure investments, it is necessary to try to ascertain whether public investment has been lacking over the past several years. From 1997 to 2007, real per capita structures (infrastructure) rose from about $19,800 to nearly $21,800, an increase of 0.95 percent per year.[9] This increase was about half of the increase in real GDP per capita over this period (1.81 percent). If the demand for public structures per person grows in tandem with

per capital real GDP growth, then U.S. infrastructure spending may have been shortchanged over this period. However, it is difficult to know definitively whether that has been the case because of recent changes in the composition of the capital stock reflecting other factors.

To see this, consider the following three categories: industrial structures, health care structures and military structures. The decline in public health care structures is perhaps surprising, but may reflect the rapid growth of spending on health care services (Medicare and Medicaid) that has come at the expense of new facilities. For military structures, the demise of the Cold War and the wars in Iraq and Afghanistan may have necessitated increased spending on armaments rather than structures.

The two largest categories—education facilities and highways—present a study in contrasts. First, the per capita stock of highways, which is the largest category, increased from just under $5,000 per person to a little more than $5,300 per person, or roughly 0.7 percent per year. This increase, however, was less than half of the growth rate in real GDP per capita and suggests some evidence that a portion of the nation's roads and highways need repairing. But does it? Recall that highway construction costs have increased sharply since 2002, undoubtedly affecting outlays.

Moreover, two other factors may be at work. First, miles driven per person age 16 and older has been declining since 2004. Second, the use of public transportation has been increasing considerably since 1995.[10] It is likely that both of these factors have been influenced by the increase in real energy prices from 2002 to 2008. Indeed, similar patterns were experienced during the oil shocks that occurred in the 1970s.

The public transportation capital stock per person has grown rapidly since 1997. Although public transit data are available only through 2006, it is likely that the rise in gasoline prices in 2007 and 2008 increased public transit usage further. If these trends continue, then it would be natural to see smaller future increases in public spending on roads and bridges.

By contrast, the stock of real public education facilities per person increased much faster than real GDP per capita over this period. Early in the post-World War II period, the baby boom necessitated a boom in school construction. The school-age percentage of the population (ages 5 to 24) rose from a little more than 31 percent in 1945 to a post World War II peak of about 38 percent in 1970. Since then, the school-age share fell to a post-WW II low of about 27.5 percent in 2007.

All else equal, this drop should slow the growth of school construction. Public education outlays, however, have increased. This increase may be due to increased outlays by state governments on college structures and may be related to the wage gap between those with a high school diploma and a college degree. With only about a third of the labor force holding a college degree, it may not be surprising to see increased expenditures on community colleges and four-year colleges.[11]

Going forward, private and public policymakers may need to think anew about how they use their scarce resources to build the nation's infrastructure of the future.[12] To take just one example, an increasing share of commerce is conducted over the Internet, which conceivably reduces the need for more traditional infrastructure facilities, such as airports and roads, while increasing the need for other types of facilities and equipment. Second, if the price of energy resumes its increase in real terms, then growth in the demand for traditional, carbon-based fuels will naturally slow or decline, and new and different kinds of alternative fuels will likely increase in use. This change would entail shifting resources to a different kind of energy infrastructure.

Finally, the retirement of the baby boomers promises to put additional strains on government budgets at all levels, as well as on the private sector. An aging population naturally requires more health-care facilities, which will necessitate increasing public outlays, likely financed either with higher taxes or with revenue originally dedicated to other areas of the budget. The result: Those who support more spending on infrastructure will face more competition for scarce resources.

Endnotes

1. It is important to distinguish between capital *stocks* and capital *flows*. The latter is the annual or quarterly change in the capital stock, otherwise known as fixed investment, which is part of GDP. This article will focus on capital stocks.

2. See Springer and Dierkers.

3. See OECD.

4. See the Texas A&M report at http://mobility.tamu.edu.

5. See Congressional Budget Office or the 2008 *Economic Report of the President*.

6. For a flavor of the debate, see Gramlich or Tatom and the references cited therein.

7. See Musgrave and Musgrave.

8. The other two duties are defense and justice (enforcement of laws). See Book III. Because of changes in the structural classification of the capital stock by the Census Bureau, measures of the capital stock in Table 1 before 1997 are not consistent with those from 1997 to the present.

9. See American Public Transportation Association. See Kolesnikova and Shimek.

10. Also see the discussion in Council of Economic Advisers, Chapter 6.

11. Shovel-ready projects are required to use at least 50 percent of the requested money within 120 days. Dollar figures in this section refer to areas in the geographic boundary of the Eighth District. Figures exclude funds approved and designated by local governments.

11

Efficiency and Private-Sector Innovation Will Improve Infrastructure

James Pethokoukis

James Pethokoukis contributes to the American Enterprise Institute as a columnist and blogger.

James Pethokoukis argues that, contrary to what many assert, America doesn't have an infrastructure crisis. He dismisses claims from Democrats of the need for expansive (and expensive) new projects. Instead, Pethokoukis maintains, America's problems could be solved by systems often used in the private sector such as increasing efficiency, providing evidence to support this assertion. Pethokoukis insists that any problems in the United States' system of infrastructure can be solved by private-sector innovation.

I f Democrats have one big economic idea, it's this: build. Crank up the infrastructure spending. Last summer, for instance, President Obama floated a "grand bargain for middle-class jobs" to cut the US corporate tax rate and use billions of dollars in revenue generated by eliminating tax breaks to fund infrastructure projects. And in his State of the Union address, he called for $50 billion in new public works spending.

But that's just a beginning. Progressives think the US suffers from a massive "public investment" deficit. They point to a much-hyped "report card" from the American Society of Civil Engineers

"Actually, America doesn't have a trillion-dollar infrastructure crisis," by James Pethokoukis, American Enterprise Institute, November 4, 2013. Reprinted by permission.

— folks who like infrastructure spending, mind you — that calls for an additional $2 trillion in spending to get US road, bridges, and water works up to a solid "B" grade from the current "D+" by 2020.

But dig a little deeper and you find claims of a supposed infrastructure crisis are wildly overstated. US public construction spending has averaged 1.8% of GDP since 1993, with a low of 1.6% in the first quarter of this year and a high of 2.2% in the second quarter of 2009. Over the past two years, it's averaged about 1.7%.

But is that a lot or a little compared to what our needs are? A Bloomberg piece last August highlights research that finds US public investment has tracked the OECD average since at least 1970. "The US. is about where it should be — close to peer nations such as Canada, Germany and Australia," concludes reporter Evan Soltas. "Nations that spend substantially more tend to be in a phase of catch-up growth, such as South Korea and Poland."

That's the view from 30,000 feet. Brookings economist and privatization advocate Clifford Winston looks at US infrastructure a bit differently. He says the lack of market forces in the transportation system — drivers, for instance, don't have to pay a special toll for driving at the heart of rush — and a government-ownership monopoly means transportation is an underpriced commodity. As he said on a recent EconTalk episode:

> I think that the claims of the infrastructure crisis are grossly overstated, and what we really have is a pricing crisis. And if we can get the prices right, that will do an awful lot to improve the condition and service of our infrastructure. ...
>
> Roads have an artificially low price. Cars are not charged for congestion, so they put pressure on peak capacity. Trucks are not charged efficiently for the damage they do to roads; they pay a gas tax when they really need to pay an explicit charge that reflects the damages they do to roads. This underpricing causes road capacity to fill up, causes the roads to wear out a lot sooner. And it generates a demand for more spending ... I say let's get the prices right. Now, the same thing is true for airports, same kind of thing; even ports. Same thing. My guess would be after getting the efficient

*prices, yeah, there probably is room for some efficient–and I mean
efficient that would satisfy cost-benefit criteria–investments in
highways in some high density areas. Certainly additional runways
in high density airports. But not the trillions of dollars that people
talk about and not nearly as much as people are led to believe. ...
We have this enormously expensive and valuable transportation
system that's the envy of the world. There's no question it's better
than other countries' systems when you look at the thing in toto.
But there's an enormous amount of waste, enormous amount of
inefficiencies in terms of operations, and for what we spend, we
could have something that's even better, and in ways that people
find hard to imagine.*

In a 2010 piece Winston outlined three big benefits from
privatizing roads and airports, apart from the billions in dollars
that would go to cash-strapped state and local governments:

*— First, private operators would have the incentive to minimize
the costs of providing transportation service and can begin the
long process of ridding the system of the inefficiencies that have
developed from decades of misguided policies.*

*— Second, private operators would introduce services and
make investments that are responsive to travelers' preferences.*

*— Third, private operators would develop new innovations
and expedite implementation of current advances in technology,
including on-board computers that can improve highway travel
by giving drivers real-time road conditions, satellite-provided
information to better inform transit riders and drivers of traffic
conditions, and a satellite-based air traffic control system to reduce
air travel time and carrier operating costs and improve safety.
The technology is there. But it hasn't been deployed in a timely
fashion because government operators have no incentive to do so.
The private sector does.*

That's right. Private-sector innovation is the answer here, not
government infrastructure banks and bullet trains with their 1960s
technology. If we want driverless cars shooting down highways
at 90 MPH — at least ASAP — it would sure help to have well-
maintained, pothole-free private roads for them to run on. The

center-right has said little on infrastructure spending recently, other than expressing opposition to more stimulus-driven spending. Conservatives have particularly missed the role of transportation as a quality-of-life issue for middle/low-income Americans. A recent study from the Equality of Opportunity Project suggests geographic isolation in areas marked by (a) sprawl and (b) poor transit systems hurts economic mobility.

But last week Senator Mike Lee, a Utah Republican, gave a big policy speech that recommended sharply cutting the federal gas tax and transferring highways authority back to the states:

> *Under our new system, Americans would no longer have to send significant gas- tax revenue to Washington, where sticky-fingered politicians, bureaucrats, and lobbyists take their cut before sending it back with strings attached. Instead, states and cities could plan, finance, and build better-designed and more affordable projects.*
>
> *Some communities could choose to build more roads, while others might prefer to repair old ones. Some might build highways, others light-rail. And all would be free to experiment with innovative green technologies, and new ways to finance their projects, like congestion pricing and smart tolls.*

We may need to spend somewhat more on infrastructure, but let's make sure we do as efficiently and intelligently as possible — and not just as a way to create more jobs.

12

Urban Planning, Digital Technology, and Smart Cities: The Future Is Near

Michel Sudarskis

Michel Sudarskis is the Secretary General of the International Urban Development Association. Sudarskis. His field of expertise is urban development.

In this viewpoint, Michel Sudarskis asserts that cities of the future will depend on digital technology and smart infrastructure. He argues that to optimize city living, urban planners will have to be sensitive to the needs of people in several key areas. Sudarskis believes combining urban planning with technology is key to the success of future cities, whether they are existing cities that are being optimized or newly constructed cities.

E conomic data indicate that the global market of technologies related to "Smart city" will reach more than $39 billions (27 billions euros) in 2016. Despite this optimism, local decision-makers are still interrogative and confused on how to address the role of large digital infrastructures in their city.

Government and business leaders recognize that the technology-enabled city is a source of sustainable growth and a powerful tool for tackling environmental and economic challenges. By unlocking technology, infrastructure and public data, cities can open up new value chains that spawn innovative applications, and

"Infrastructure for the rise of smart cities?" by Michel Sudarskis, International Urban Development Association. Reprinted by permission.

information products that make possible sustainable modes of city living and working. While smart initiatives are underway in urban centers around the world, most cities have yet to realize the enormous potential value from integrated, strategically- designed smart infrastructure. Through clear vision and leadership, civic leaders and executives can help cities make the transition to initiatives that maximize the smart city value opportunity.

The city has always been conceived as a place of exchange; with the use of the digital technology a smart city increases the intensity of exchange, of networking and communication, which are the basic elements of city life and economy. Digital technology and infrastructure could be the point of entry of new social and economic ambitions: it is a social issue as it involves the collective and democratic participation of users (*social networks*); it is a political issue that questions management and urban governance and its evolution; it is a technical question with the exponential growth of information technologies (*cloud computing, big data*).

Optimization of the Existing City by Digital Technology

There is no doubt that the city driven by smart infrastructure can generate new applications and information services that enable different lifestyles and work. However, infrastructures alone are not sufficient. They need "intelligence" to remain efficient. Digital technology is a factor of change in the sense of shifting from an infrastructure-led logic to a service-led economy. Developing smart infrastructure against a backdrop of dwindling public finance means being honest about why technology is being introduced, which may shift the focus rather to improving the essential systems of urban services, than providing smarter technology across the board.

Making cities smart requires other elements such as a vision of their future, and here what matters is not technology *per se,* but the image people have on key issues: *climate* change, how will we *live* tomorrow; *work*: seamless integration from home to working places - *leisure*: where and how the world comes to you - *life*: longer, easier and highly personalised - *home*: the heart of modern living; etc. Some refers to the use and dissemination of digital technology as a source of employment in disadvantaged neighbourhoods, favouring access to employment and vocational training, and being a facility instrument in the process of democratic representation and participation in civic life. Obviously this is a restrictive approach, but with the merit to draw attention to the soft dimension of the "smart city" process next to the infrastructure-led approach.

The Manufacture of the City by (with) Digital Technology

Digital technology leads to rethink the process of urban development, in order to build better connected housing and neighbourhoods, improve public spaces, foster inhabitants' relationship towards a smarter and more productive city; beyond transport, businesses and education, a digital plan must also focus on improving the state of play for urban living by offering new services to residents. Digital technology enables among other effects a shift in the political relationship between citizens and the policy system: from complaining (traditional political attitude) to listening (via internet or other digital devices) and then to direct and immediate participation (via social networks). It enables also the reduction in the number of intermediaries in daily life (internet booking is the case), supporting practices empowerment and spontaneity.

Today, public funding is under pressure. To reduce costs, including public service costs, local authorities will externalise more and more city services such as accounting, human resources and information, in order to maintain essential services such as education and social support. In these times of rigor, local authorities should make a strong analysis of profitability of their investments in smart products and processes as this will lead to the generalization of capital costs borne by the private sector, coupled with long-term concession for the management of the service.

Finally, urban planning evolution under digital pressure means working towards collective intelligence by the presence of the user, via the digital system, in public decision making. If "educating" end-users is needed to ensure citizens' empowerment, it is necessary also to accompany elected officials who need the skills to anticipate the development of their territory and the role of digital services.

13

Local Control of Infrastructure Can Make a Big Difference

Charles Marohn

Charles Marohn is a civil engineer, urban planner, and founder and president of the nonprofit media organization Strong Towns.

Charles Marohn asserts that the cost of infrastructure and public projects has gotten way out of control and analyzes how this came to pass. Marohn compares this situation to that of healthcare and makes several recommendations, citing ways in which he believes change could be brought about for the good of all, including pursuing infrastructure projects primarily on the local level and considering the various means of funding projects.

A few weeks ago I finished the book *Catastrophic Care: Why Everything We Think We Know about Health Care is Wrong* by David Goldhill. In 400 pages he shed more light for me on our health care system than the hundreds of hours I've spent informing myself about health care policy. In fact, the book was so illuminating, after reading it I felt dumb for having previously wasted so much time. If nothing in our health care conversation today makes sense to you and you wish it did, you have to read this book.

"This is why infrastructure is so expensive," by Charles Marohn, Strong Towns, June 5, 2017. https://www.strongtowns.org/journal/2017/6/4/this-is-why-infrastructure-is-so-expensive. Licensed under CC BY SA 3.0.

One of Goldhill's key devices is to place the language and values of the health care industry on a metaphorical island. He constantly talks about life "on the island" and "on the mainland." For example, on the island, nobody ever talks about prices, they only talk about costs. This is not a subtle nuance. Prices, of course, are related to costs but, in a true competitive marketplace — one where people, not a third party, actually pay directly for the goods and services they consume — we never talk in terms of costs. Only prices.

Does it really matter to you how much it costs the grocery store to provide that twelve pack of your favorite beverage? Of course not. It's only matters to you — someone living on the mainland — what the price is to you. Price is how you determine your preferences among competing items. Profit is how the market receives feedback on those preferences. High prices invite substitution. High profits invite competitors. This is all basic and obvious to us on the mainland.

Which is why, on the healthcare island, the conversation is about costs. Your preferences don't matter, except where they are aligned with the objectives of those on the island. Substitution doesn't matter; there are no competing services. Obscene profit margins don't invite competitors; they invite consolidation. Justifying costs to third party payers, instead of prices to patrons, is the name of the game. It's a bizarre world that doesn't make any sense to people like Goldhill when they take a critical look at it.

Last week, Bloomberg's Noah Smith wrote an article titled "The U.S. Has Forgotten How To Do Infrastructure" that asked a lot of questions that would get us to a Goldhill like analysis of our infrastructure approach. Just like on Healthcare Island, on Infrastructure Island we have our own way of talking about things. And we never talk about prices, only about costs. And as Smith suggests, costs go up and nobody seems to understand why.

He goes through and dismisses all of the usual suspects. Union wages drive up infrastructure costs (yet not true in countries paying equivalent wages). It's expensive to acquire land in the property-rights-obsessed United States (yet countries with weaker eminent domain laws have cheaper land acquisition costs). America's too spread out or our cities are too dense (arguments that cancel each other out). Our environmental review processes are too extensive (yet other advanced countries do extensive environmental reviews with far less delay). I concur with all these points, by the way.

Smith concludes with this:

> *That suggests that U.S. costs are high due to general inefficiency — inefficient project management, an inefficient government contracting process, and inefficient regulation. It suggests that construction, like health care or asset management or education, is an area where Americans have simply ponied up more and more cash over the years while ignoring the fact that they were getting less and less for their money. To fix the problems choking U.S. construction, reformers are going to have to go through the system and rip out the inefficiencies root and branch.*

Much like health care, our infrastructure incentives are all wrong. Until we fix them — until we go through the system and rip out the inefficiencies root and branch — throwing more money at this system is simply pouring good money after bad. Let me provide some examples.

The more lane miles a state has, the more federal transportation dollars that state qualifies for. What is the incentive? It is, of course, to build more lane miles. Add to this the fact that federal transportation programs generally pay 90%+ for new construction, but only ~50% for maintenance, and we have a system that encourages states to build more than they can ever maintain.

That's okay. When we put together our appropriation request, is it better to show a catastrophic level of need or is it better to prudently ask for only what is absolutely necessary? It's an altogether silly question; the more desperate we can make ourselves and the more miserable we can make taxpayers, the more they will demand that governments pay more for infrastructure.

In the United States, many engineering contracts — and if not the contracts, at least the cost estimates — are based on a percentage of construction costs. Imagine getting your car's oil changed and the industry-wide cost for the labor was a percentage of the oil cost. As you can well imagine, the price of oil for cars would skyrocket, one way or another (we can imagine a specialty line of oil exclusive to cars). The bigger the project, the more everyone involved gets paid. Thus: big, expensive projects.

In addition, the longer the project takes, the more everyone gets paid. Change orders — because of weather, redesign, special requests, etc... — often add to project costs and, even when they don't, take time ($$) to administer. Once a government commits to a project, they are committing to an open checkbook. That check will be written in a system where nearly everyone involved will be compensated more the longer the project takes and the more expensive it becomes.

Back when I did engineering work, I worked on two separate contracts for very similar projects at roughly the same time. Project A was for a city, while Project B was being paid for by a developer. For Project A, we signed a lump sum contract with the city to do the study and design and then an hourly billing schedule for inspection. For Project B, we had an hourly agreement with the developer to provide the same services. Guess who paid less in the end (and it wasn't even close).

At times, the developer was in my office twice a day getting updates, checking on progress and overseeing my work. My engineering was a huge expense for him. When he got my bill, he demanded hourly itemization and scrutinized the entire thing, refusing to pay when he thought things shouldn't have taken as long as they did. It was a pain and I remember being annoyed, but I also remember it got done quickly and for a tiny fraction — my admittedly faulty memory is telling me 1/3 the cost — of what a very similar project cost the public client.

In Minnesota where I live, public contracts are required to always take the lowest bid price. This creates incentives for all kinds of shenanigans. I worked on one state paving project where the low bidder bid most every item far below cost except for bituminous, where they were the highest price by many multiples.

The strategy for executing the contract was then clear: Do the least amount necessary to fulfill the contract agreement and overrun the bituminous as much as possible. An extra 1/8 of one inch of pavement over a 40 mile project — an amount hardly perceptible — caused a massive cost overrun.

I could go on, but here's the crazy thing: On *Infrastructure Island*, this all makes sense. Nobody there is really unethical, it's just that the incentives have perverted what, in other realms, would be seen as normal and acceptable. Make the project big. Make it take a long time. Create a lot of overruns. Don't maintain it until it falls apart catastrophically. Few on *Infrastructure Island set out to do these things, but they happen and nobody loses a lot of sleep over it. That›s because, for the players involved, there is little negative feedback and lots of positive feedback associated with these perverse outcomes.*

I think it would be easy to say at this point that the only way to deal with this is a purely libertarian approach; privatize it all and make people pay to use it. I don't think things are that easy and I would not recommend that approach for a variety of reasons.

Here's what I do recommend. First, I think we need to find every opportunity to localize infrastructure spending and funding. Instead of giving cities money, we need to give them many more tools for raising their funds locally. I'd take little off the table. Cities have far more incentives than other levels of government to put money to work prudently, especially when they must confront their own constituents who are directly paying the bill. Cities should be spending more money on data analysis than on lobbyists, more money on figuring out what works than where they get more money. (Note: I'd reduce state and federal taxes along with this to make it, at least initially, revenue neutral.) Not to get political, but President Trump's infrastructure plan — which is sure to have at least some bipartisan support — is almost certain to be an epic disaster of bad incentives.

Second, the only tool I would take off the table — or at least constrain — is debt. Cities should have the ability to take on cash flow take and make strategic investments with debt, but they should not be able to live beyond their means today — intentionally or not — at the expense of future generations. I'd cap municipal debt service at 5% of locally-generated revenue with the ability to go up to 10% with approval of voters. No city should have the capacity to blow themselves up financially.

Third, I'd encourage all cities to adopt infrastructure funding mechanisms that provide the most direct feedback. A sales tax to pay for roads is popular for the same reasons it is destructive: because it's indirect and results in an unfocused slush fund. Tolls, maintenance districts and direct user fees are less popular but actually more empowering for people in that it allows them to speak their preferences more forcefully and clearly.

Finally, while I wouldn't privatize infrastructure, I would push for more contracts that are design/build/warranty instead of splitting those into two separate but colluding contracts — design and build — with the taxpayers getting struck with the long term warranty. If we can align the incentives of the players involved, we can build infrastructure that is actually necessary, and while doing it quicker and at lower prices than we do now.

14

Compared to Other Developed Countries, US Infrastructure Is Outdated

Hiba Baroud

Hiba Baroud is an assistant professor of civil and environmental engineering. Baroud specializes in analyzing risk, resilience, and the reliability of infrastructure systems.

In this viewpoint, Hiba Baroud analyzes the deficits of the United States' infrastructural systems compared to those of other developed countries. Baroud focuses on areas of potential improvement, including updating infrastructure to protect against disruptive weather and increasing sustainability and smart infrastructure. With countries like Switzerland, Germany, Finland, and Norway leading the way to innovative and resilient infrastructure, the United States would do well to follow their lead.

How does infrastructure in the U.S. compare to that of the rest of the world? It depends on who you ask.

On the last two report cards from the American Society of Civil Engineers, U.S. infrastructure scored a D+. This year's report urged the government and private sector to increase spending by US$2 trillion within the next 10 years, in order to improve not only the physical infrastructure, but the country's economy overall.

"U.S. Infrastructure Needs Resilience, Sustainability," by Hiba Baroud, The Conversation, August 3, 2017. https://theconversation.com/measuring-up-us-infrastructure-against-other-countries-78164. Licensed under CC BY ND 4.0.

Meanwhile, the country's international rank in overall infrastructure quality jumped from 25th to 12th place out of 138 countries, according to the World Economic Forum.

On Feb. 12, the White House revealed its $1.5 trillion plan to rebuild U.S. infrastructure, financed through a combination of federal, local and private sectors. This is a long awaited plan, as the nation's infrastructure quality continues to suffer.

The quality of infrastructure systems can be measured in different ways – including efficiency, safety and how much money is being invested. As a researcher in risk and resilience of infrastructure systems, I know that infrastructure assessment is far too complex to boil down into one metric. For instance, while the U.S. ranks second in road infrastructure spending, it falls in 60th place for road safety, due to the high rate of deaths from road traffic.

But by many measures, the U.S. falls short of the rest of the world. Two of these characteristics are key to our infrastructure's future: resilience and sustainability. A new class of solutions is emerging that, with the right funding, can help address these deficiencies.

Resilience

Resilient infrastructures are able to effectively respond to and recover from disruptive events. The U.S. is still in the top 25 percent of countries with the most resilient infrastructure systems. But it falls behind many other developed countries because the country's infrastructure is aging and increasingly vulnerable to disruptive events.

For example, the nation's inland waterway infrastructure has not been updated since it was first built in the 1950s. As a result, 70 percent of the 90,580 dams in the U.S. will be over 50 years old by 2025, which is beyond the average lifespan of dams.

In addition, since the 1980s, weather-related power outages in the U.S. have become as much as 10 times more frequent.

Several European countries – such as Switzerland, Germany, Norway and Finland – are ahead of the U.S. in the FM Global Resilience Index, a data-driven indicator of a country's ability to respond to and recover from disruptive events. Though these countries are exposed to natural hazards and cyber risks, their infrastructure's stability and overall high standards allow them to effectively survive disruptive events.

The U.S. infrastructure was built according to high standards 50 years ago, but that's no longer enough to ensure protection from today's extreme weather. Such weather events are becoming more frequent and more extreme. That has a severe impact on our infrastructure, as cascading failures through interdependent systems such as transportation, energy and water will ultimately adversely impact our economy and society.

Take 2016's Hurricane Matthew, which was considered a 1,000-year flood event. The unexpectedly strong rainfalls broke records and caused damages equivalent to $15 billion. A better infrastructure that is modernized and well-maintained based on data-driven predictions of such events would have resulted in less impact and faster recovery, saving the society large damages and losses.

As the country's infrastructure ages, extreme weather events have a greater impact. That means the recovery is slower and less efficient, making the U.S. less resilient than its counterparts.

Sustainability

In terms of sustainability practices designed to reduce impact on human health and the environment, the U.S. does not make it to the top 10, according to RobecoSAM, an investment specialist focused exclusively on sustainability investing.

Average CO_2 emissions per capita in the U.S. are double that of other industrialized countries and more than three times as high as those in France.

The infrastructure in most EU countries facilitates and encourages sustainable practices. For example, railroads are mostly dedicated to commuters, while the bulk of freight moves through waterways, which is considered the most cost-effective and fuel-efficient mode of transportation.

In the U.S., however, 76 percent of commuters drive their own cars, as railroads are mostly reserved for freight and public transit is not efficient compared to other countries. American cities do not show up in the top cities for internal transportation, as do cities such as Madrid, Hong Kong, Seoul and Vienna.

To promote sustainable practices, global initiatives such as the New Climate Economy and the Task Committee on Planning for Sustainable Infrastructure aim to guide governments and businesses toward sustainable decision-making, especially when planning new infrastructure.

Smart Infrastructure As a Solution

To address challenges of resilience and sustainability, future infrastructure systems will have to embrace cyber-physical technologies and data-driven approaches.

A smart city is a city that is efficient in providing services and managing assets using information and communication technology. For example, in Barcelona, a city park uses sensor technology to collect and transmit real-time data that can inform gardeners on plant needs.

While there is no official benchmark to grade countries in this aspect, a number of American cities, such as Houston and Seattle, are considered among the world's "smartest" cities, according to economic and environmental factors.

In order to prioritize dam restoration, the dam safety engineering practice is moving toward a data-driven process that would rank the dams based on how important they are to the rest of the waterway system. And last year, the U.S. Department of Transportation issued a call to action to improve road safety by releasing a large database on road fatalities, which researchers can study to answer important questions.

Similarly, worldwide initiatives are seeking smart solutions that integrate communication and information technology to improve the resilience of cities such as 100 Resilient Cities and Smart Resilience.

It's imperative that we pursue these types of new solutions, so U.S. infrastructure can better and more sustainably withstand future disruptions and deliver better quality of life to citizens, too. Perhaps, by addressing these needs, the U.S. can improve its score on its next report cards.

15

Similar Economic Benefits in US and Indian Historical Railroad Development

Dave Donaldson

Dave Donaldson is an economist and professor of economics at Stanford University.

Dave Donaldson analyzes the historical railroad development in the US and India, looking at the economic impact it had on each country. He provides evidence that details the economic benefits attained by both countries as a result of their railroad systems. However, Donaldson cautions that it may not be applicable to high-cost infrastructure systems today. Nonetheless, he considers it to be a useful case study in the potential economic benefits of investment in transportation infrastructure.

Many governments commit significant portions of their budgets to building and maintaining transportation infrastructure. For example, nearly 20 percent of the money lent from the World Bank to developing countries is earmarked for transportation infrastructure projects, which is more than education, health and social services combined. Some of these projects, such as the Interstate Highway System in America or the National Trunk Highway System in China, are breathtaking achievements of engineering. But the costs of projects like these are also breathtaking, and their economic benefit is often unclear.

Recent research finds that the economic benefits of transportation infrastructure investment can be significant.

To measure some of these benefits I analyzed two of the most ambitious transportation projects in history: the building of the vast railroad system in India by the British government from 1870 to 1930 and the dramatic expansion of the railroad network in America from 1870 to 1890.

This work measures three key features of the Indian and American experience with railroad expansion:

1. Investment in railroad infrastructure significantly reduced the costs of trading goods.
2. Improved railroad infrastructure increased the volume of goods shipped.
3. The economic benefits of increased railroad access greatly outweighed the construction costs.

The result of this historical analysis suggests that the economic gains from transportation infrastructure can be substantial. And the true economic impact may not be known until years after a project is completed. Naturally, it is important to use caution when generalizing these conclusions to validate present-day infrastructure proposals that may not have the same outcome on expanding trade.

Nonetheless, the historical examples from India and America clearly illustrate the economic benefits that are possible when nations invest soundly in their transportation infrastructure.

Railroad Infrastructure Reduced Trade Costs

Measuring the true costs of trade can be difficult since transportation users rarely record the full economic costs of a journey. It's not simply the price of the journey, but other aspects such as trip duration and the risk of damage or delay along the way. To account for such costs, I drew on the theory of market arbitrage, which states that if an identical product is selling for different prices in two geographic locations, then the price gap would be equal to the total cost of moving the product between those two locations.

Colonial India provides a rare example of a setting in which it is relatively easy to learn from arbitrage when it came to trade in salt. Due to the heavy regulation of salt production by the British government in Northern India, distinct varieties of salt were produced in just a few locations. One can estimate how much it cost to move goods like salt by comparing the prices of such salt varieties across points in space where salt was consumed. By comparing trade costs before and after the journey, we can see how the new railroad network helped to reduce the costs of moving goods.

Access to the railroad allowed remote locations in India to cheaply trade with the rest of India and the world. Trade via railroads was less expensive than road trade – goods could be shipped 800 km by rail for the same price as 100 km by road. Rail trade could also occur for the same price at four times the distance of water-based (river or coastal) trade.

The case of America's railroads was similar. Extensive research by Robert Fogel (1964) tracked the full costs of transporting various goods by rail and its alternatives, and per his calculations, railroad trade was significantly less expensive than trade by road, but not substantially cheaper than water-based trade like India. This is not surprising given the impressive waterborne navigation facilities and technologies available in the U.S. in the late nineteenth century. The advantage of railroads came from their proliferation throughout the much of the country, reaching a density of transportation corridors far beyond what was available by water.

Railroad Infrastructure Increased the Shipment of Goods

Railroads clearly reduced the cost of trading and the access to low-cost routes. But did these lower costs lead to much increased trade among transportation users? To answer this question in the case of India (where the provision of intra-national trade data made this possible) I estimated the "trade elasticity", the proportion by which trade flows grew as trade costs fell. The Indian trade data imply that this elasticity is about four – for every percentage reduction in trade costs, the volume of trade would rise by about four percent. While this method for estimating trade costs was only obtained for one commodity – salt – there was a pronounced response of trade to railroads in all commodities.

The Economic Benefits of Railroad Access

Measuring the economic benefits of railroad access is challenging because of potential "spillover effects", which can be both positive and negative.

Though it is tempting to compare the evolution outcomes over time in similar regions that gained rail access with those that did not (a standard difference-in-differences approach), such a comparison would only isolate the relative fortunes of the two regions without accounting for any positive or negative spillovers from one region onto the other.

For instance, a region without rail access could see its own transport costs fall when a neighboring region gains railroad access, or it could be that the increased prosperity in the region with rail access creates greater demand for the products of its neighboring regions, including those far from the railroad. These positive spillovers will lead the estimate of relative effects to be smaller than it would be in the absence of spillovers. Thus the economic benefits would be underestimated, both because we would estimate only a small relative effect, and also because we would fail to capture the additional positive effect on regions without direct access.

Spillover effects can also be negative, for instance when regions compete against one another for finite demand for their products. A region's privileged access to transport facilities allows it to sell its products more cheaply in third markets than is profitable for regions far from the rail network, and this inflicts economic harm on regions without rail access. These negative spillovers mean that the measured relative effects will be particularly large, yet the true effect will have been quite small since the negative spillover effect on the area without rail access goes unaccounted for.

Since the nature of transportation infrastructure projects like railroads involves connecting regions to one another, properly calculating the positive and negative spillover effects is an important consideration when measuring the overall economic impact.

The Gravity Model

Progress can be made in isolating the spillover effects of transportation infrastructure by drawing on insights from the powerful "gravity" model of trade, which shows that bilateral trade flows are proportional to the size of the two trading economies and (inversely) to their distance from one another. For example, large regions tend to buy proportionally more goods and services from their neighbors. The model also assumes that:

i. Trade is balanced, since sellers are unlikely to export goods without getting imports of equal value in return; and

ii. Markets clear, since there cannot be more of any good consumed in the world than what was produced.

The gravity model stands on firm empirical and theoretical footing and has been used to accurately predict trade flows between countries for a variety of goods and services. This footing can be used to derive a methodology for estimating the impact of transportation infrastructure that would be purged of the positive and negative spatial spillovers. This method effectively draws on the assumption that the gravity model is a useful approximation to real-world trading behavior in order to guide an analysis of how regional interactions, via trade, create spillovers of infrastructure projects.

An additional prediction of gravity models is that there should be a stable relationship between the economic welfare in any region and its "market access", a variable that summarizes how connected a region is to all other locations. Studying this relationship provides a way to measure the effect of railroads on economic welfare that excludes spillover effects since spillovers take place within the market access variable.

In this model, positive and negative spillovers of railroad access are present – so a location with railroad access can have a positive or negative impact on non-railroad locations. Since all spillovers either increase or decrease the non-railroad locations' market access measure, what regional economies value is not railroad access per se, but instead, the market access that railroads generate.

An additional and testable implication of this prediction is that market access should act like a "sufficient statistic" for the impact of railroads on real GDP. Once a market access is accounted for, there should be no additional measured effect of railroad access on real GDP.

When observing the railroad network in India, I estimated that in a typical district, the arrival of railroad access caused real Gross Domestic Product (GDP) in the agricultural sector (the largest sector of India's economy at that time) to increase by around 17 percent. There is also striking evidence in favor of the sufficient statistic prediction in this context.

In the case of the U.S., there is no historical measure of local GDP, but a powerful alternative is the value of land in a location. In settings where most factors of production (capital and workers) are geographically mobile, the benefits of residing in a location will be capitalized into the value of land. My estimates with my colleague, Richard Hornbeck, imply that a counterfactual 1890 U.S. economy without railroads would have seen a 60 percent reduction in the value of aggregate farmland.

In this setting, there is some evidence that counties benefited from railroad access even after accounting for their benefits of market access. This violates the gravity model's sufficient statistic prediction and suggests that railroads enacted change in local economies above and beyond what is encompassed in the model. Future work could explore this finding by building a similar concept to market access for a less parametric version of the gravity model.

The historical railroad projects in India and the U.S. demonstrate sizable economic benefits. In both cases, benefits were substantially larger than the project construction costs. In the case of the U.S., the benefits were much larger than the hypothetical system of extended canals that were a plausible alternative use of the funds spent on railroads. These estimated benefits focus only on the short-term movement of goods and ignore the positive outcomes on mobility of people, capital, and ideas, implying actual benefits might even be greater.

While these are only two historical case studies, and extrapolating from them to a full understanding of the returns of modern-day investments cannot be done without great care, these lessons from history teach us not to underestimate the economic benefits of transportation infrastructure.

16

What Are the Costs of Underinvestment in Infrastructure?

Samuel Sherraden and Shayne Henry

Samuel Sherraden is a policy analyst in the Economic Growth Program at the New America Foundation. He has lived in East Asia for numerous years and is interested in the Chinese economy. Shayne Henry practices commercial law as an associate at Keker, Van Nest & Peters. Prior to attending law school, he was a research associate for the New America Foundation's Economic Growth Program.

In this viewpoint, Samuel Sherraden and Shayne Henry make the argument that underinvestment in infrastructure negatively impacts individuals, businesses, and governments in a number of ways. Through looking at the losses caused by infrastructure deficits in monetary figures and other specific statistics, the authors concretely emphasize the importance of updated and well-maintained infrastructure.

Under-investing in infrastructure carries costs for households, businesses, and the government by increasing maintenance, wasting time, and allocating resources inefficiently. These costs reduce efficiency and impede economic growth.

Quantifying Efficiency Loss

Bottlenecks and traffic delays in our ground and air transportation systems are paralleled by inefficiencies across many modes of infrastructure. According to various estimates from government institutions and non-profits organizations, the efficiency lost because of poor infrastructure is probably in excess of $195 billion per year and would be higher if it included private infrastructure networks, such as freight rail or telecommunications, and infrastructure networks that are regulated largely by states and municipalities, such as ports and inland waterways.

Roads

Americans wasted 4.8 billion hours in traffic in 2009.[1] These delays resulted in the waste of 3.9 billion gallons of fuel. Fuel loss alone cost truckers $33 billion, a significant addition to shipping costs for producers. The delays are most acute in the largest metropolitan areas, including Washington, D.C., Chicago, and Los Angeles, where travelers spend an average of 70, 70, and 63 hours per year in traffic at an average cost per passenger of over $1,500.

Congestion has worsened as the expansion of the highway system has failed to keep pace with usage. Since 1980, mileage of U.S. highways increased 4.5% while the number of passenger cars increased 12.7% and the number of trucks increased 56.4%. As a result, the amount of time wasted has increased dramatically over the past few decades rising from 14 hours per driver in 1982 to 34 hours in 2009. The cost of these delays has increased from $24 billion in 1982 to $115 billion in 2009 dollars. Congestion has also slowed truck freight. Truckers experience 243 million hours of bottleneck delay annually at a cost of $32.15 per hour, in addition to general traffic delay.[2] Given that oil prices have increased dramatically in recent years, and are likely to remain elevated, the cost of congestion and poor infrastructure are rising.

Aviation

Delays on the ground are matched by delays in the air. In 2009, 21% of flights were delayed, down slightly from the 2007 rate of 24%, the highest rate of flight delays in Federal Aviation Administration (FAA) history.[3] According to the Joint Economic Committee, these flight delays cost a cumulative $40.7 billion and wasted 740 million gallons of fuel.[4] A slightly more conservative study sponsored by the FAA found that flight delays negatively impact the economy by $32.9 billion per year, at a cost to travelers of $16.7 billion in 2007 alone.[5] Although air traffic and flight delays have moderated since 2007, without capacity expansion flight delays will likely rise again as air traffic grows.

Clean Water

Poor infrastructure is costing Americans not only when they travel, but also when they stay at home. America's water pipes are old, ranging in age from 50 to 100 years.[6] In 1980, the Environmental Protection Agency notes that 10% of water pipes were already in "poor, very poor, or life elapsed" condition. The Agency expects this number to increase to 45% of all piping by 2020. Further, as pipes age they begin to deteriorate at an exponential rate. If left unaddressed, the funding gap for clean water and drinking water is projected to increase to $122 billion and $102 billion, respectively. The American Recovery and Reinvestment Act allocated $13.5 billion to water infrastructure, but that is a drop in the metaphorical bucket compared to current needs.[7] Water systems lose between 6 and 25 percent of their water through leaks and breaks, wasting over 7 billion gallons of water each day.[8]

Public Housing

The U.S. Public housing stock also faces a staggering amount of unfunded capital needs. According to the Department of Housing and Urban Development, more than $20 billion is currently needed to rebuild and update America's public housing portfolio.[9] While the American Recovery and Reinvestment Act allocated $4 billion to address this need, that total falls far short of even conservative estimates of needed repairs and renovations.

Public Safety

The broken-down state of America's infrastructure also has high human costs. The most notable failure was the breaking of the levees during Hurricane Katrina, which contributed to the death of 1,800 people. Greater infrastructure investment would have prevented this tragedy and cost far less than the human and capital cost of the flooding that followed the hurricane. In 1998, there was a comprehensive $14 billion plan to buttress the Southern Louisiana levee system by rebuilding the region's protective wetlands, but it was scuttled by Congress due to cost concerns. In addition to the staggering loss of life, Hurricane Katrina caused between $150 and $200 billion in damage. These estimates do not include the loss of more than environmental and resource damage caused by flooding, and the far-reaching implications of the loss of the natural wetland barrier.[10]

Infrastructure affects the safety and well-being of Americans even in the absence of natural disasters. The collapse of the I35W Mississippi River Bridge in Minneapolis, Minnesota in 2007 had nothing to do with the weather. Although the bridge had been categorized as "structurally deficient" as the result of inspections in 1990 and was considered "in need of replacement" in 2005, investment shortfalls resulted in a decision to wait to replace the bridge until 2020, despite the fact that the bridge carried 140,000 vehicles each day.[11] The collapse in 2007 resulted in the death of 13 people and the injury of 145 others.

Aside from bridge collapses, which may seem extraordinary, reports find that poorly maintained roads may contribute up to a third of all highway fatalities, or more than 14,000 deaths every year.[12] Poor infrastructure also manifests in less noticeable dangers to public safety. Water contamination due to broken seals, leaking pipes and deteriorating reservoirs have been attributed to outbreaks of salmonella such as the occurrence that killed one person and sickened 442 others in Alamosa, Colorado in 2008.[13]

Conclusion

The American economy, in aggregate as well as at the individual level, is paying a heavy cost for its aging and deteriorating infrastructure. From wasted fuel to wasted time, lost lives and lost revenue, there is an obvious need to address the economic efficiency gap resulting from poor roads, antiquated air traffic control systems, and other out-of-date infrastructure. Ignoring America's crumbling infrastructure will only serve to slow an economy that is in the early stages of recovery, and leave the future of American growth on shaky ground.

Notes

1 Urban Mobility Report 2010. Texas Transportation Institute. December 2010. Available Online. http://tti.tamu.edu/documents/mobility_report_2010.pdf

2 An Initial Assessment of Freight Bottlenecks on Highways. U.S. Department of Transportation. Federal Highway Administration. 6.0 Conclusions and Recommendations. October 2005. Available Online. http://www.fhwa.dot.gov/policy/otps/bottlenecks/chap6.htm

3 Air Travel Consumer Report. U.S. Department of Transportation. Office of Aviation Enforcement and Proceedings. March 2010. Available Online. http://airconsumer.dot.gov/reports/2010/March/2010MarchATCR.pdf

4 our Flight Has Been Delayed Again. A Report by the Joint Economic Committee Majority Staff. May 2008. Available Online. http://jec.senate.gov/public/?a=Files.Serve&File_id=47e8d8a7-661d-4e6b-ae72-0f1831dd1207

5 Total Delay Impact Study. The National Center for Excellence for Aviation Operations Research. October, 2010. Available Online. http://www.isr.umd.edu/NEXTOR/pubs/TDI_Report_Final_10_18_10_V3.pdf

6 U.S. Environmental Protection Agency. The Clean Water and Drinking Water Infrastructure Gap Analysis. 2002. Available Online. http://www.epa.gov/ogwdw/gapreport.pdf

7 Foley & Lardner LLP. Water Infrastructure Funding in the ARRA. March 23, 2009. Available Online. http://www.foley.com/publications/pub_detail.aspx?pubid=5844

8 U.S. Drinking Water Challenges in the Twenty-First Century. Levin, Ronnie B., Paul R. Epstein, Tim E. Ford, Winston Harrington, Erik Olson, and Eric G. Reichard. Environmental Health Perspectives 110 (suppl 1): 43-52. 2002. Available Online. http://www.win-water.org/win_news/021402article.html and Drinking Water. Report Card for America's Infrastructure. American Society of Civil

Engineers. 2009. Available Online. http://www.infrastructurereportcard.org/fact-sheet/drinking-water

9 U.S. Department of Housing and Urban Development. Transforming Rental Assistance. Written testimony of Shaun Donovan, Secretary of the U.S. Department of Housing and Urban Development. May 25, 2010. Available Online. http://portal.hud.gov/hudportal/documents/huddoc?id=hud_testimony_5-25-10.pdf

10 Patrick Jonsson. Christian Science Monitor. Private Dollars Leading Recovery of New Orleans. June 27, 2007. Available Online. http://www.csmonitor.com/2007/0627/p01s06-usec.html and
Mark L. Hicks & Michael J. Burton. Marshall University: Center for Business and Economic Research. Hurricane Katrina: Preliminary Estimates of Commercial and Public Sector Damages. September, 2005.

11 Minnesota Department of Transportation. Downtown Minneapolis Traffic Volumes. 2006. Available Online. http://www.dot.state.mn.us/traffic/data/maps/indexmaps/2006/mplsin.pdf. Retrieved August 7, 2007.

12 Thomas J. Donohue. Speech. Rebuilding America- The Time is Now! Irving, Texas. August 10, 2007.

13 Colorado Department of Public Health and Environment. Waterborne Salmonella Outbreak in Alamosa, Colorado March and April 2008. Outbreak Identification, Response, and Investigation. November 2009. Available Online. http://www.cdphe.state.co.us/wq/drinkingwater/pdf/AlamosaInvestRpt.pdf and
David Olinger. The Denver Post. Hazards in the Water. March 22, 2009. Available Online. http://www.denverpost.com/news/ci_11968325

17

The Federal Government Could Improve Infrastructure

Charles Marohn

Charles Marohn is a civil engineer, urban planner, and founder and president of the nonprofit media organization Strong Towns.

This viewpoint takes the form of a letter from Charles Marohn—a civil engineer and urban planner—to the President of the United States, Donald Trump. In this letter Marohn makes the case for increased federal infrastructure spending. He explains why state and local governments are unable to cover the costs of infrastructure maintenance and improvement on their own. Finally, he offers suggestions for how to make infrastructure projects manageable, including focusing on maintaining existing infrastructure over constructing new infrastructure and keeping closer tabs on spending.

Dear Mr. President,

I am writing you on behalf of our Board of Directors and our membership regarding a potential surge in federal infrastructure spending. At Strong Towns, we have developed a unique understanding that allows us to speak with a level of clarity on this issue. Our supporters have no financial interest in whether or not more federal money is spent on infrastructure;

"A letter to POTUS on infrastructure," by Charles Marohn, Strong Towns, January 23, 2017. https://www.strongtowns.org/journal/2017/1/22/a-letter-to-potus-on-infrastructure. Licensed under CC BY-SA 3.0.

our mission is to advocate for ways those investments can make our cities stronger.

To borrow a real estate term, America's infrastructure is a nonperforming asset. For nearly every American city, the ongoing cost to service, maintain and replace it exceeds not only the available cash flow but the actual wealth that is created.

For example, we did a deep financial study of the city of Lafayette, Louisiana. We found that the city had public infrastructure — roads, streets, sewer, water, drainage — with a replacement cost of $32 billion. In comparison, the total tax base of Lafayette is just $16 billion. Imagine building a $250,000 home and needing an additional $500,000 in infrastructure to support it. This seems incredible. But not only is it common, it is the default for cities across America.

This imbalance is caused by incentives we embed in our current approach. When the federal government pays for a new interchange or the extension of utilities, local governments gladly accept that investment. The city, while spending little to no money of their own, has an immediate cash benefit from the jobs, permit fees and added tax base. The only thing the local government must do is promise to maintain the new infrastructure, a bill that won't come due for decades.

Here's the catch: when we look at that bill, our cities almost always can't pay it. Cities never run a return-on-investment analysis that includes replacement costs. Cities never even compute the tax base needed to financially sustain the investment. There's no incentive to do it and every reason not to.

In psychological terms, this is called temporal discounting. The people running local governments, as well as the people they serve, have the natural human tendency to highly value free money today and deeply discount, if not altogether dismiss, the financial burden these projects will create in the future. We've been building infrastructure this way for two generations. We have created a lot of short term growth, but we've also created trillions of dollars of non-performing assets, infrastructure investments that are slowly bankrupting our cities, towns, and neighborhoods.

The fundamental insolvency of our infrastructure investments is the root cause of the pension crisis and the explosion in municipal debt. It is the real reason why our infrastructure is not being maintained. New growth is easy and comes with all kinds of cash incentives. Maintenance is difficult and has little upside. Cities with huge maintenance backlogs still prioritize system expansion because they are chasing the short-term cash benefits of new growth, even at the expense of their future solvency.

What do we do today? To paraphrase former Defense Secretary Donald Rumsfeld, we're going to make investments in infrastructure with the systems we have, not the ones we wish we had. There are ways to get better results now.

- We need to prioritize maintenance over new capacity. With so many non-performing assets, it's irresponsible to build additional capacity. Project proposers will try to add additional capacity with their maintenance projects. If it is truly warranted, it can and should be funded locally. Cities need to discover ways to turn such investments into positive ROI projects, a process the federal government can only impede.

- We must prioritize small projects over large. Small projects not only spread the wealth, they have much greater potential for positive returns with far lower risk. Large projects exceed their budgets more often and with greater severity — dollars and percentage — than smaller projects. A thousand projects of a million dollars or less have far more financial upside than a single billion-dollar project ever will. It's administratively easier to do fewer, big projects, but that is a bureaucratic temptation we need to overcome.

- We should spend far more below ground than above. Many of our sewer and water systems are approaching 100 years old. When these core pipes fail, the problems cascade throughout the system. Technology may soon dramatically change how we use our roads and streets making investments in expansion there obsolete, but water and sewer will still flow

through pipes as it has for thousands of years. We should
spend at least $5 below ground for every $1 we spend above.

- We should prioritize neighborhoods more than 75 years old.
We've modeled hundreds of cities across the country and in
every one the neighborhoods with the highest investment
potential are the ones that existed before World War II. These
are established places where small investments have a huge
impact. Most investments in neighborhoods built after World
War II are simply bailouts, pouring good money after bad.

Small maintenance projects focusing on below ground
infrastructure in old, established neighborhoods have the greatest
potential for positive returns. These projects will put people to work,
create jobs and fix failing infrastructure as well as, if not better than,
the large expansion projects currently in the shovel ready backlog.
These are also the kind of projects that get private capital off the
sidelines and back to work building wealth in our communities.

In addition, while we understand that a surge in infrastructure
spending is not going to wait for systematic reform, there are some
modest — yet transformative — reforms we can make as part of
this process.

- Require states and municipalities receiving funds to do
accrual accounting. Governments must have a real accounting
of their long-term liabilities, including infrastructure, on
their balance sheet. The days of fake financial statements
that ignore government's long term promises needs to end.
- Require municipalities to account for infrastructure as an
accruing liability instead of a depreciating asset. Cities have
an obligation to maintain infrastructure. It's improper to
pretend infrastructure is an asset that loses value as it ages.
Like pensions, infrastructure is an inter-generational promise
that is properly accounted for as a liability.
- Require project applicants to do a *financial* return on
investment. Many federal programs currently require an ROI

analysis, but the emphasis is on non-monetary, social returns. These are fine as secondary criteria, but infrastructure projects need to make financial sense. Municipalities must know what kind of revenue stream is needed to maintain an infrastructure investment over multiple life cycles.

Finally, we believe you should consider the channels through which federal funds are distributed. There is strong evidence to suggest that working directly with mayors to fund local projects creates the greatest potential for innovation as well as the highest fiscal returns. Money given directly to state transportation departments should have a heavy emphasis on maintenance. We would avoid funding counties and other regional entities which, we have found, tend to build the lowest-returning of all infrastructure projects.

Thank you for your consideration. If we can be of assistance to you or your team in this matter, please do not hesitate to contact me.

Sincerely,

Charles L. Marohn, Jr. PE AICP

Professional Engineer, Certified Planner

Founder and President of Strong Towns

18

President Trump's Infrastructure Plan Won't Save America's Infrastructure

Eileen Appelbaum

Eileen Appelbaum is Co-Director at the Center for Economic and Policy Research and a visiting professor in the department of management at the University of Leicester in the United Kingdom.

In this viewpoint, Eileen Appelbaum argues that the infrastructure plan proposed by President Trump in his 2018 State of the Union address would have a disastrous effect on America's infrastructure. Appelbaum asserts that the plan would lead to major cuts in infrastructure spending at a time when greater investment is needed, and the move away from federal funding would harm state and local governments. Through breaking down what the plan proposes, Appelbaum is able to convey the potential negative effects.

In his January State of the Union address, President Trump called for $1.5 trillion in infrastructure spending over the next decade. If that amount materialized, it could go a long way toward meeting the nation's infrastructure needs. But the release on February 12 of his detailed plan for raising and allocating those funds dashed any hope that this administration would address the nation's acute need for infrastructure investment.

"Trump's Plan Won't Solve the Problems of America's Crumbling Infrastructure," by Eileen Appelbaum, Center for Economic and Policy Research, February 15, 2018. http://cepr.net/blogs/cepr-blog/trump-s-plan-won-t-solve-the-problems-of-america-s-crumbling-infrastructure. Licensed under CC BY 4.0.

The meagerness of the federal contribution — just $200 billion over ten years, or less than 0.1 percent of GDP over that period — was already clear from the State of the Union. Half of those funds are allocated to an Incentive Program intended to support surface transportation and airports, passenger rail, ports and waterways, flood control, water supply, hydropower, water resources, drinking water facilities, wastewater facilities, storm water facilities, and brownfield and Superfund sites. Just listing everything the President's plan claims to address for a federal expenditure of just $100 billion makes the inadequacy of the plan obvious. But there's more.

The Incentive Program requires states and localities to put up 80 percent of the cost of any project in order to get a federal match of 20 percent. This turns the traditional approach to infrastructure investment on its head. The federal government typically provides 80 percent of the funding for such projects. It is wishful thinking to imagine how cash-strapped states and cities — already on the hook for extensive local infrastructure spending — will be able to find new public sources of financing, especially now that the recent Republican-passed tax law has severely limited their ability to raise taxes to pay for such undertakings.

Trump's plan turns infrastructure investment on its head in another way as well. Traditionally, the selection of projects to be funded by the federal government emphasized benefits to the public. The administration's plan weighs the ability to attract sources of funding outside the federal government at 70 percent when considering whether to support it; economic and social returns from the project count for just 5 percent. Federal funding will go to projects that are most attractive to private investors, rather than to those, like clean water, that meet the needs of communities.

President Trump's plans for the nation's infrastructure are, unbelievably, even worse than they appear. In the President's budget, released on the same day as the infrastructure plan, Democrats in Congress identified more than $240 billion over the next decade in proposed cuts to ongoing infrastructure. This includes a cut of $122 billion to the Highway Trust Fund as well as reductions in programs that fund rail, aviation, and wastewater projects. Net federal spending on infrastructure may actually fall over the next decade if the President's plans are approved by Congress, potentially leaving the nation's infrastructure in a more dire condition than when he took office.

Public-Private Partnerships and the Role of Private Equity

With states and localities sidelined by budget realities, the administration appears to be counting on private investors to step-up and propose public-private partnerships. No doubt some projects will attract private financing. The infrastructure plan sweetens such deals by:

- Allowing private investors to recoup their costs and earn profits by placing tolls on existing interstate highways where they are currently restricted;
- Making it easier for large- and mid-sized airports to charge higher passenger fees and extend these fees to small airports;
- Turning rest stops on interstates into commercial areas that can charge for anything except drinking water and toilets; and
- Allowing fees for the use of public recreational water facilities.

Increased tolls and fees paid by the public would go to private investors that engage in partnerships with public agencies.

Private equity (PE) firms increased fundraising for infrastructure investment following Trump's election. As an advisor to the Trump campaign, private equity mogul (now Commerce Secretary) Wilbur Ross promulgated a no-lose, high-return plan for private equity investment in infrastructure. Shortly after Trump's inauguration, Joe Baratta, global head of private equity at Blackstone Group, the largest private equity firm in the world, announced plans to raise an infrastructure fund of as much as $40 billion in equity. This would be Blackstone's largest fund ever. Global Infrastructure Partners did raise $15.8 billion for what is currently the largest infrastructure fund. Brookfield Asset Management Inc. raised $14 billion for its third infrastructure fund. In 2017, PE firms raised a record amount of money — nearly $40 billion, not counting the Blackstone fund that is still in process — for infrastructure investment; PE funds now hold $70 billion for this purpose.

Little of Ross' proposal, that would have secured high returns for private equity investors, has survived in the plan put forward by President Trump. In spite of two years of fundraising, it's unclear how much PE will contribute to the 80 percent mix of state, local and private funds needed to qualify for federal funds. Adding to the murky role PE will play in infrastructure investment, the return expectations for infrastructure investment have actually come down, and experienced PE investors generally expect a 10 to 11 percent return on investment for core infrastructure strategies.

Moreover, absent strong guarantees of outsized earnings, PE infrastructure funds prefer to buy existing public assets, rather than invest in developing new infrastructure. This may explain the bizarre and unexpected proposals in President Trump's budget to sell Dulles and Reagan National airports, the Baltimore–Washington and George Washington Parkways, the Tennessee Valley electric power assets, and so much more government-owned infrastructure.

What is clear is that the public will pay for local infrastructure projects carried out under the $100 billion Incentive Program, whether financed by state and local governments alone, or via public-private partnerships, through fees, tolls, and possibly higher gasoline taxes. The needs of poorer communities unable to raise much money will largely go unmet.

Other Provisions in the Infrastructure Plan

In addition to the $100 billion Incentive Program, another $50 billion would be allocated to the Rural Infrastructure Program, 80 percent of it in the form of block grants to states to be used in rural areas with populations of less than 50,000 and for Tribal and territorial infrastructure. This is just $5 billion a year spread across the entire United States. Another $20 billion would be made available for Transformative Projects. These grants would be administered by Ross' Department of Commerce and would cover 30 to 80 percent of the costs of these projects, depending on whether the funds were requested for a demonstration project, project planning, or capital construction.

One element of the infrastructure plan has survived since it was first proposed during Trump's presidential campaign: the plan will gut environmental protection requirements that date back to the 1970s. Under rubrics such as "streamlining the application process" or "getting projects completed more quickly," roads, bridges, and pipelines will be constructed without the necessary protections for clean air, clean water, and the environment. Some projects would be allowed to proceed before completion of a review by the National Environmental Protection Act. Local communities would not know the environmental impacts they will face and will have little opportunity for input during project planning.

Organizations to Contact

The editors have compiled the following list of organizations concerned with the issues debated in this book. The descriptions are derived from materials provided by the organizations. All have publications or information available for interested readers. The list was compiled on the date of publication of the present volume; the information provided here may change. Be aware that many organizations take several weeks or longer to respond to inquiries, so allow as much time as possible.

American Enterprise Institute (AEI)
1789 Massachusetts Avenue, NW
Washington, DC, 20036
phone: (202) 862-5800
website: http://www.aei.org/

The American Enterprise Institute is a public policy think tank that sponsors independent research and dedicates work to building a safer and freer world. Its research, reporting, and materials support issues that surround the topic of infrastructure.

American Society of Civil Engineers (ASCE)
1801 Alexander Bell Drive
Reston, VA, 20191
phone: (800) 548-2723
website: http://www.asce.org/

The American Society of Civil Engineers is an organization representing members of the civil engineering profession. Civil engineering involves planning, designing, constructing, and operating the built environment or infrastructure. The ASCE publishes information including a report (every four years) that gives a grade to US infrastructure.

Association for the Improvement of American Infrastructure (AIAI-Infra)
1430 Broadway #1106
New York, NY 10018
phone: (516) 277-2950
email: readytowork@aiai-infr.org
website: www.aiai-infra.info

The Association for the Improvement of American Infrastructure was created with the goal of moving public-private partnerships (P3s) forward to better support America's infrastructure. It serves as a resource for industry leaders, legislators, and municipal officers to promote infrastructure growth and sustainability.

Brookings Institution
1775 Massachusetts Ave. NW
Washington, DC, 20036
phone: (202) 797-6000
website: https://www.brookings.edu/

The Brookings Institution is a nonprofit organization that is concerned with public policy. The Institute conducts research aimed at solving problems of great concern for society. The Institute publishes a variety of online and print materials covering a range of topics including infrastructure concerns.

Global Infrastructure Investor Association (GIIA)
Hays Galleria
1 Hays Lane
London SE1 2RD
United Kingdom
phone: +44 (0)203-440-3922
email: info@giia.net
website: http://giia.net

The Global Infrastructure Investor Association plans and delivers a program of global advocacy and stakehold engagement to encourage private investment in infrastructure around the world. It facilitiates engagement between private investors and governments to contribute funds to build and manage infrastructure.

International Urban Development Association(INTA)
18 rue Daval
75011
Paris, France
phone: +33 1 58 30 34 52
website: https://inta-aivn.org/en/

The International Urban Development Association is a global membership organization dedicated to bringing public and private policymakers together to share resources that may benefit urbanized areas.

National Transportation Safety Board (NTSB)
490 L' Enfant Plaza, SW
Washington, DC, 20594
phone: (202) 314-6000
website: https://www.ntsb.gov/Pages/default.aspx

The NTSB is an independent US Federal Government Agency. It is concerned with the area of transportation in the United States and consequently provides information concerning transportation infrastructure.

Reason Foundation
5737 Mesmer Ave.
Los Angeles, CA, 90230
phone: (310) 391-2245
website: https://reason.org/

The Reason Foundation is a nonprofit organization dedicated to advancing a free society and public policy research. Through online and print resources, the Foundation highlights various issues in the US including transportation and associated infrastructure.

Strong Towns
1511 Northern Pacific Rd. Rm 206
Barinerd, MN, 56401
phone: (844) 218-1681
website: https://www.strongtowns.org/

Strong Towns is a nonprofit organization that supports a particular development model for America's towns, cities, and neighborhoods. The organization believes that transportation is a big factor and reports on issues of significance to cities, towns, and neighborhoods.

US Department of Homeland Security (DHS)
Secretary of Homeland Security
Washington, DC, 20528
phone: (202) 282-8000
email: DHSSecretary@hq.dhs.gov
website: https://www.dhs.gov/

One function of the US Department of Homeland Security is to monitor infrastructure. This governmental agency is charged with maintaining national policies to secure and strengthen the sixteen infrastructure sectors that are critical for the public health, safety, and security of the United States.

US Trade and Development Agency (USTDA)
1101 Wilson Blvd., Suite 1100
Arlington, VA, 22209
phone: (703) 875-4357
website: https://www.ustda.gov/

The USTDA helps support economies around the world by outsourcing jobs and services to developing economies. The agency funds projects and partnerships by supporting sustainable infrastructure in countries around the globe.

US Transport and Infrastructure Committee (T&I)
US House of Representatives
2251 Rayburn House Office Building
Washington, DC, 20515
phone: (202) 225-9446
email: Transport@mail.house.gov
website: https://transportation.house.gov/

The US Transport and Infrastructure Committee has the important job of overseeing all issues of transportation and infrastructure in the US, including maritime and water, aviation, highways, railroads, bridges, and mass transit. T&I is invested in protecting America's infrastructure.

Bibliography

Books

Claire Barratt. *The Spotter's Guide to Urban Engineering: Infrastructure and Technology in the Modern Landscape.* Buffalo, NY: Firefly Books, 2011.

Brian Brenner. *Don't Throw This Away!: The Civil Engineering Life.* Reston, VA: American Society of Civil Engineers, 2007.

Deborah Cadbury. *Dreams of Iron and Steel: Seven Wonders of the Nineteenth Century, From the Building of the London Sewers to the Panama Canal.* New York, NY: Fourth Estate, 2004.

Roger H. Grant. *Railroads and the American People.* Bloomington, IN: Indiana University Press, 2012.

Derek Hayes. *The First Railroads: Atlas of Early Railroads.* Buffalo, NY: Firefly Books, 2017.

Edward Humes. *Door to Door: the Magnificent, Maddening, Mysterious World of Transportation.* New York, NY: Harper, 2016.

Will Jones. *New Transport Architecture.* London, UK: Mitchell Beazley, 2006.

Rosabeth Moss Kanter. *Move: Putting America's Infrastructure Back in the Lead.* New York, NY: W. W. Norton & Company, 2015.

Richard Lacayo. *Man-Made Wonders: How They Did It: The Design Secrets of the World's Greatest Structures.* New York, NY: Time Books, 2012.

Matthys Levy. *Engineering the City: How Infrastructure Works: Projects and Principles for Beginners.* Chicago, IL: Chicago Review Press, 2000.

Tom Martinson. *The Atlas of American Architecture: 2000 years of Architecture, City Planning, Landscape Architecture and Civil Engineering.* New York, NY: Random House, 2009.

Paul McCaffrey. *U.S. Infrastructure.* Hackensack, NJ: H. W. Wilson Co., 2011.

Henry Petroski. *The Road Taken: The History and Future of America's Infrastructure.* New York, NY: Bloomsbury, 2016.

Annalise Silivanch. *Rebuilding America's Infrastructure.* New York, NY: Rosen Publishing, 2011.

George Sullivan. *Built to Last: Building America's Amazing Bridges, Dams, Tunnels, and Skyscrapers.* New York, NY: Scholastic Nonfiction, 2005.

Christian Wolmar. *The Great Railroad Revolution: The History of Trains in America.* New York, NY: Public Affairs, 2012.

Periodicals and Internet Sources

Jennifer Agiesta, "CNN/ORC poll: Most back boost in infrastructure spending, oppose growing military budget," *CNN*, March 8, 2017. https://www.cnn.com/2017/03/08/politics/donald-trump-poll-spending-defense-infrastructure/index.html

Liz Collin, "The Whole Bridge Is Down': 1st Responders Reflect On 35W Bridge Collapse," *CBS Minnesota*, July 26, 2017. http://minnesota.cbslocal.com/2017/07/26/bridge-collapse-firefighters/

Bryce Covert, "Trump's infrastructure plan would end up costing many Americans," *ThinkProgress*, November 10, 2016. https://thinkprogress.org/trump-infrastructure-6d3ba097b24b/

Joseph Erbentraut, "America's Water Infrastructure Is In Absolutely Terrible Shape," *HUFFPOST*, January 16, 2017.

https://www.huffingtonpost.com/entry/us-water-safety_
us_56bcf122e4b0b40245c5d388

Jason Gold, "No More Bumps in the Road," *US News & World Report*, November 18, 2014. https://www.usnews.com/ opinion/economic-intelligence/2014/11/18/public-private-partnerships-can-help-rebuild-americas-infrastructure

Brittany Grayson, "The Man Who Predicted the Bridge Collapse. Kind Of," *Discover*, August 2, 2007. http:// discovermagazine.com/2007/aug/man-who-predicted-the-bridge-collapse

Merrit Kennedy, "Lead-Laced Water In Flint: A Step-By-Step Look At The Makings Of A Crisis," *NPR*, April 20, 2016. https://www.npr.org/sections/thetwo-way/2016/04/20/465545378/lead-laced-water-in-flint-a-step-by-step-look-at-the-makings-of-a-crisis

Alison Kosik, "Experts: U.S. water infrastructure in trouble," *CNN*, January, 21, 2011. http://www.cnn.com/2011/ US/01/20/water.main.infrastructure/index.html

Stephen Loiaconi, "Experts: Miami Bridge Collapse 'Terrifying' but 'Incredibly Rare,'" WJLA Washington, DC, March 16, 2018. http://wjla.com/news/nation-world/experts-miami-bridge-collapse-terrifying-but-incredibly-rare

Aarian Marshall, "How Not to Screw Up Spending $1 Trillion on US Infrastructure," *Wired*, January 30, 2017. https:// www.wired.com/2017/01/not-screw-spending-1-trillion-us-infrastructure/

Joe McCarthy, "Infrastructure disasters in US show how hard development really is," *GLOBALCITIZEN*, January 7, 2016. https://www.globalcitizen.org/en/content/infrastructure-disasters-in-us-show-how-hard-devel/

Lisa McKinney, "Building Resilience," *Capitol Ideas*, March/ April 2018.

Tim Newcomb, "50 States, 50 Things America Must Fix Now," *Popular Mechanics*, January 26, 2017. https://www.popularmechanics.com/technology/infrastructure/g2932/50-states-infrastructure/

Brad Plumer, "Donald Trump's infrastructure plan wouldn't actually fix America's infrastructure problems," *VOX*, November 18, 2016. https://www.vox.com/policy-and-politics/2016/11/16/13628382/donald-trump-infrastructure-plan

Hilary Russ, "America's infrastructure $1.44 trillion short through 2025: report," *Reuters*, May 10, 2016. https://www.reuters.com/article/us-usa-infrastructure/americas-infrastructure-1-44-trillion-short-through-2025-report-idUSKCN0Y12K6

Andrew Soergel, "Is U.S. Infrastructure Destined to Crumble?" *US News & World Report*, March 15, 2016. https://www.usnews.com/news/the-report/articles/2016-03-15/ask-an-economist-is-americas-infrastructure-destined-to-crumble

Erik Sofge, "The 10 Pieces of U.S. Infrastructure We Must Fix Now," *Popular Mechanics*, April 6, 2008. https://www.popularmechanics.com/technology/infrastructure/g85/4257814/

Greg Uyeno, "Lessons From 10 of the Worst Engineering Disasters in US History," *LIVESCIENCE*, August 2, 2016. https://www.livescience.com/55619-engineering-disasters.html

Index